Shadows and Light

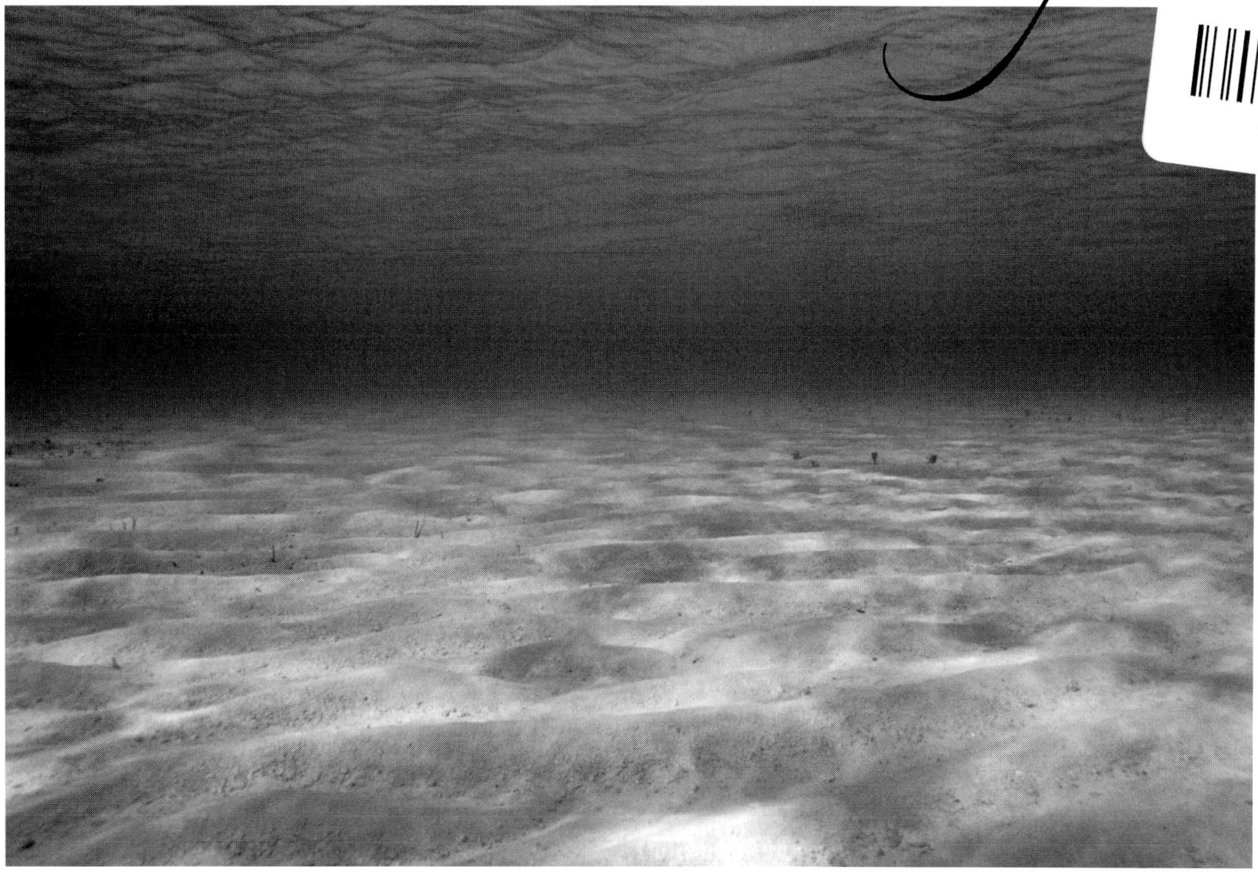

A Photographic Exploration of the Sea in Black and White

To Matt & Liz –
See you in
Bikini Bottom!

JONATHAN BIRD

Published by Jonathan Bird Photography
www.jonathanbird.net

Printed in the United States of America
by United Graphics, Incorporated.

Limited Edition First Printing

ISBN 0-9728634-0-0

To Christine

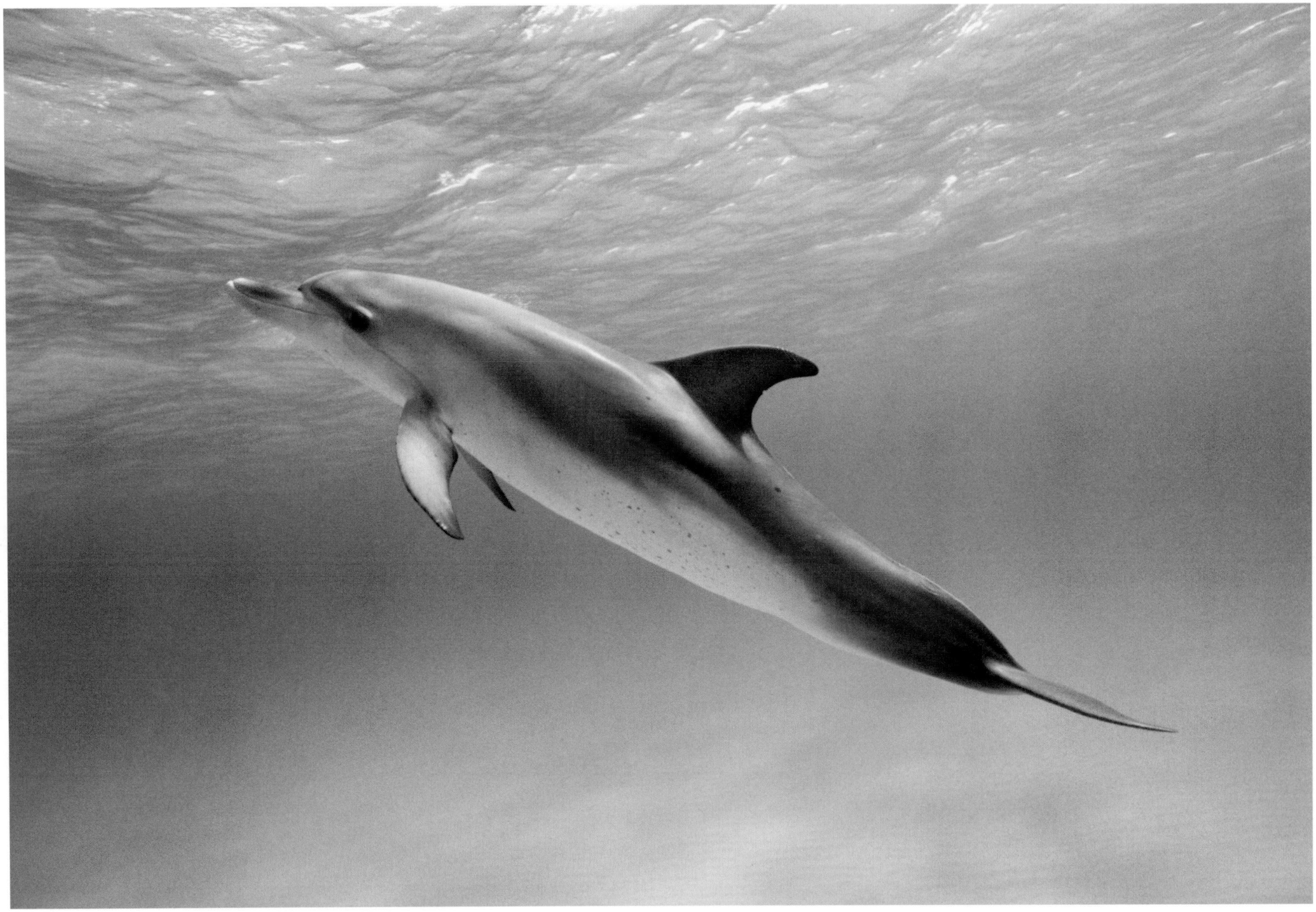

Atlantic Spotted dolphin, Little Bahama Bank, Bahamas

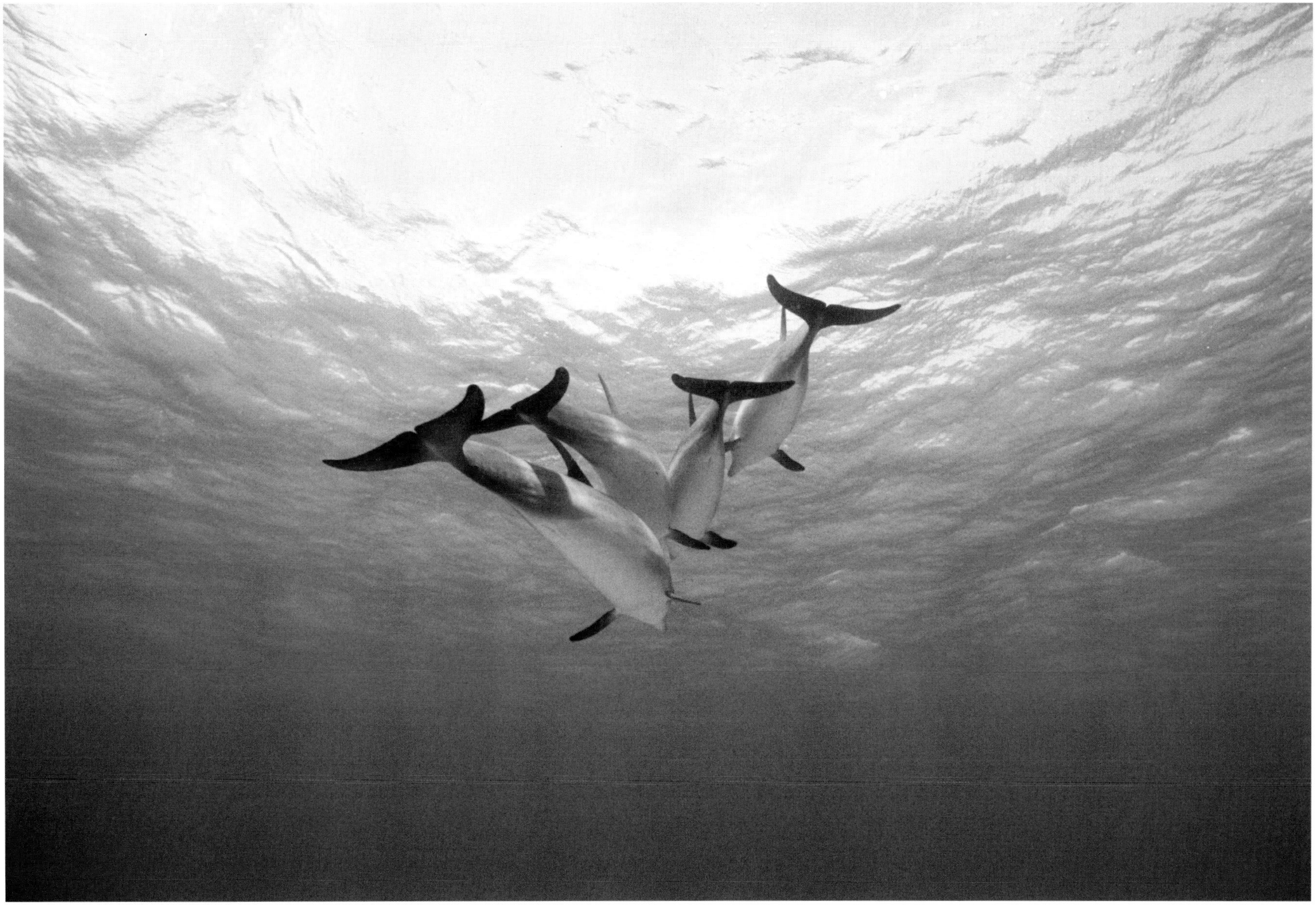

Atlantic Spotted dolphins, Little Bahama Bank, Bahamas

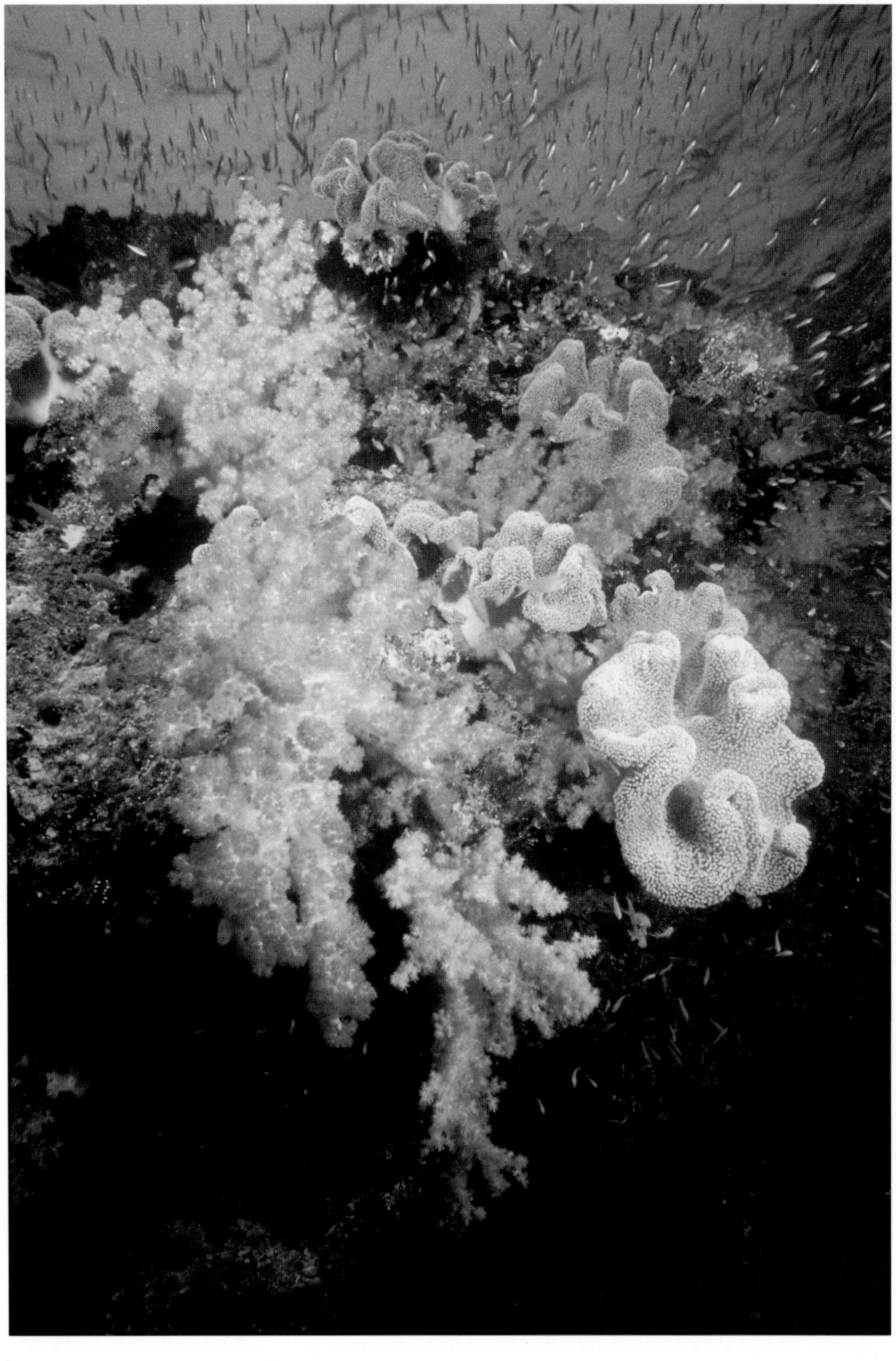

Soft coral on reef, Fiji

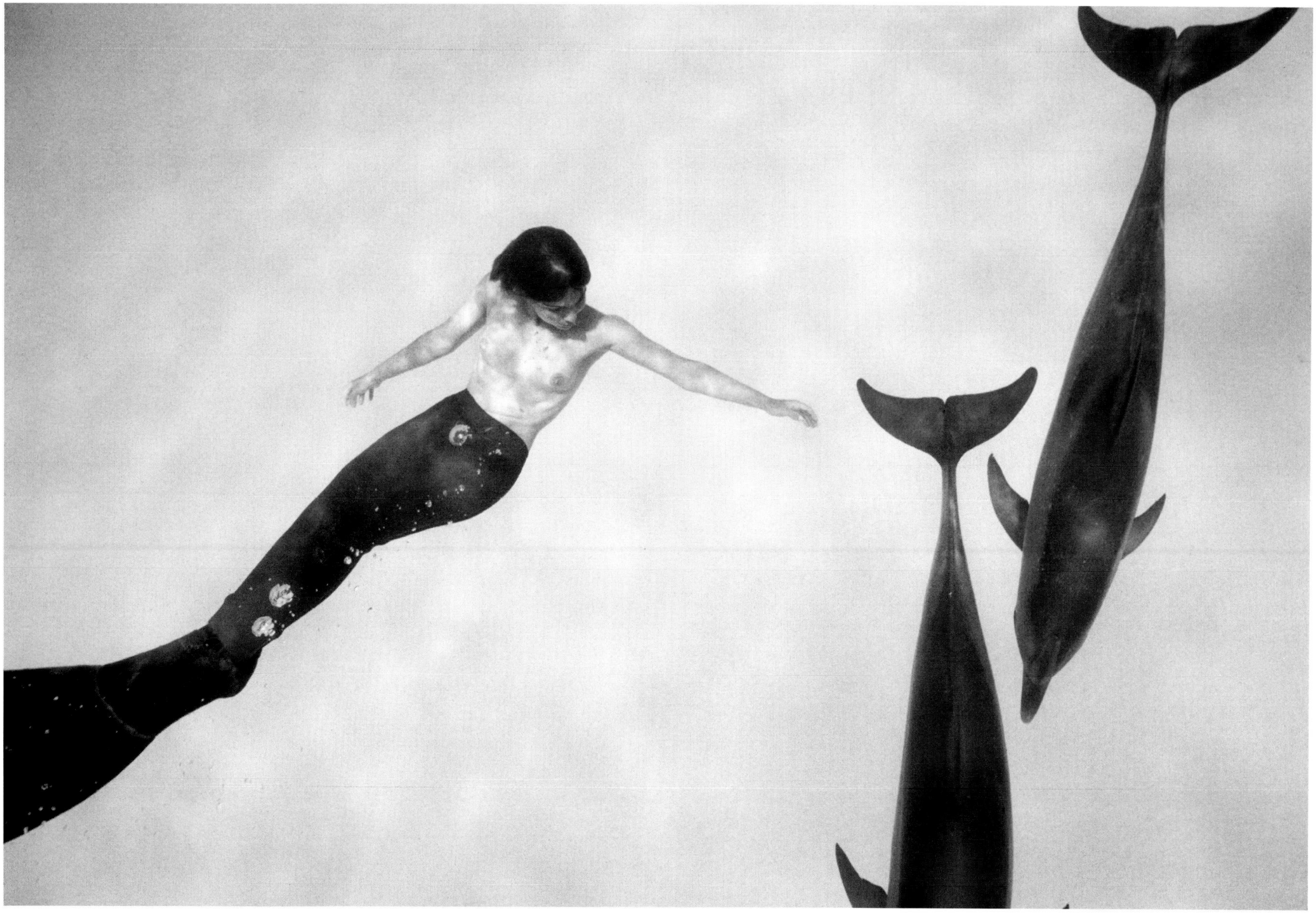

Mermaid with Atlantic Spotted dolphins, Bahamas

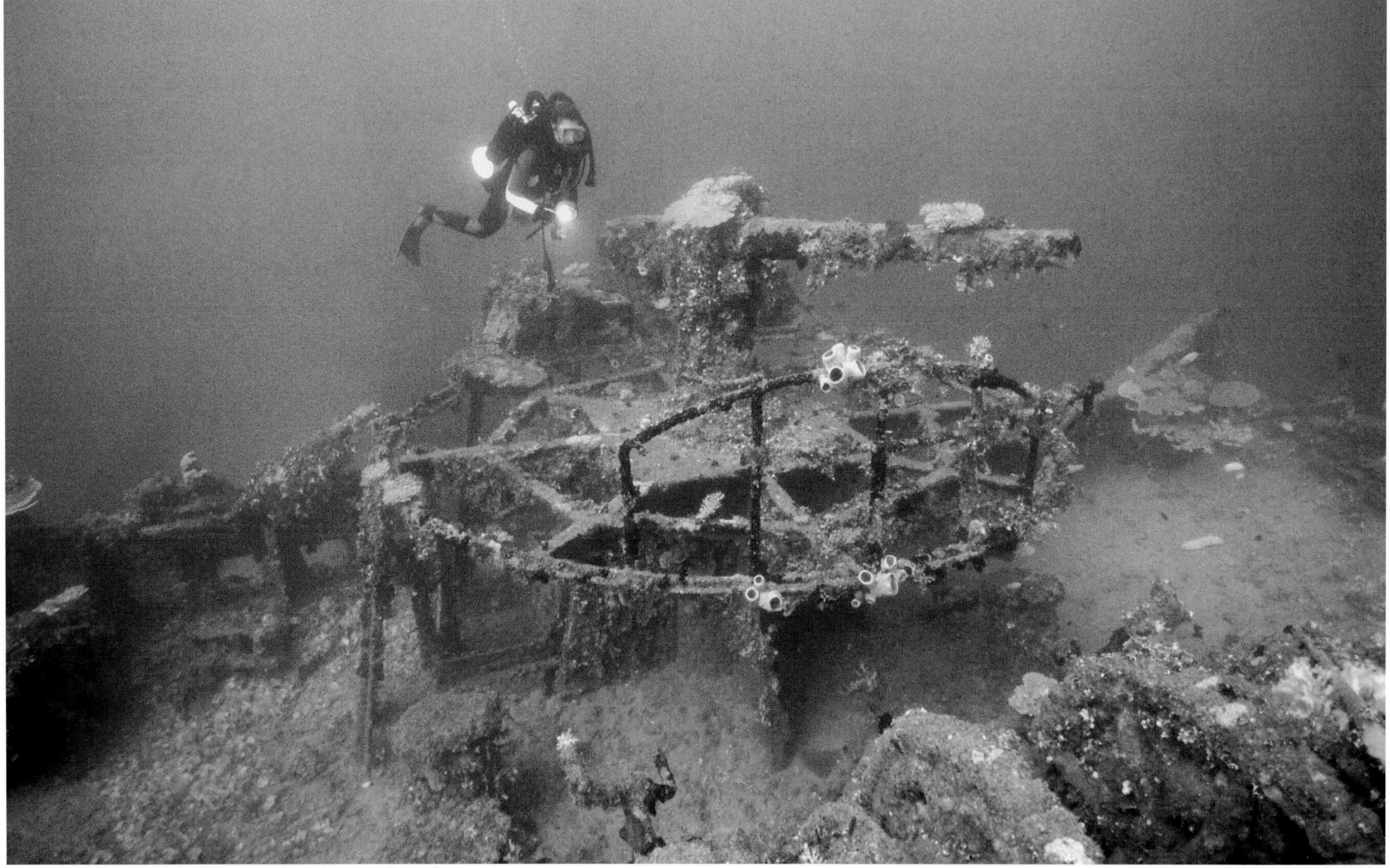

Bow gun of the Asakazi Maru, Kwajalein Atoll, Marshall Islands

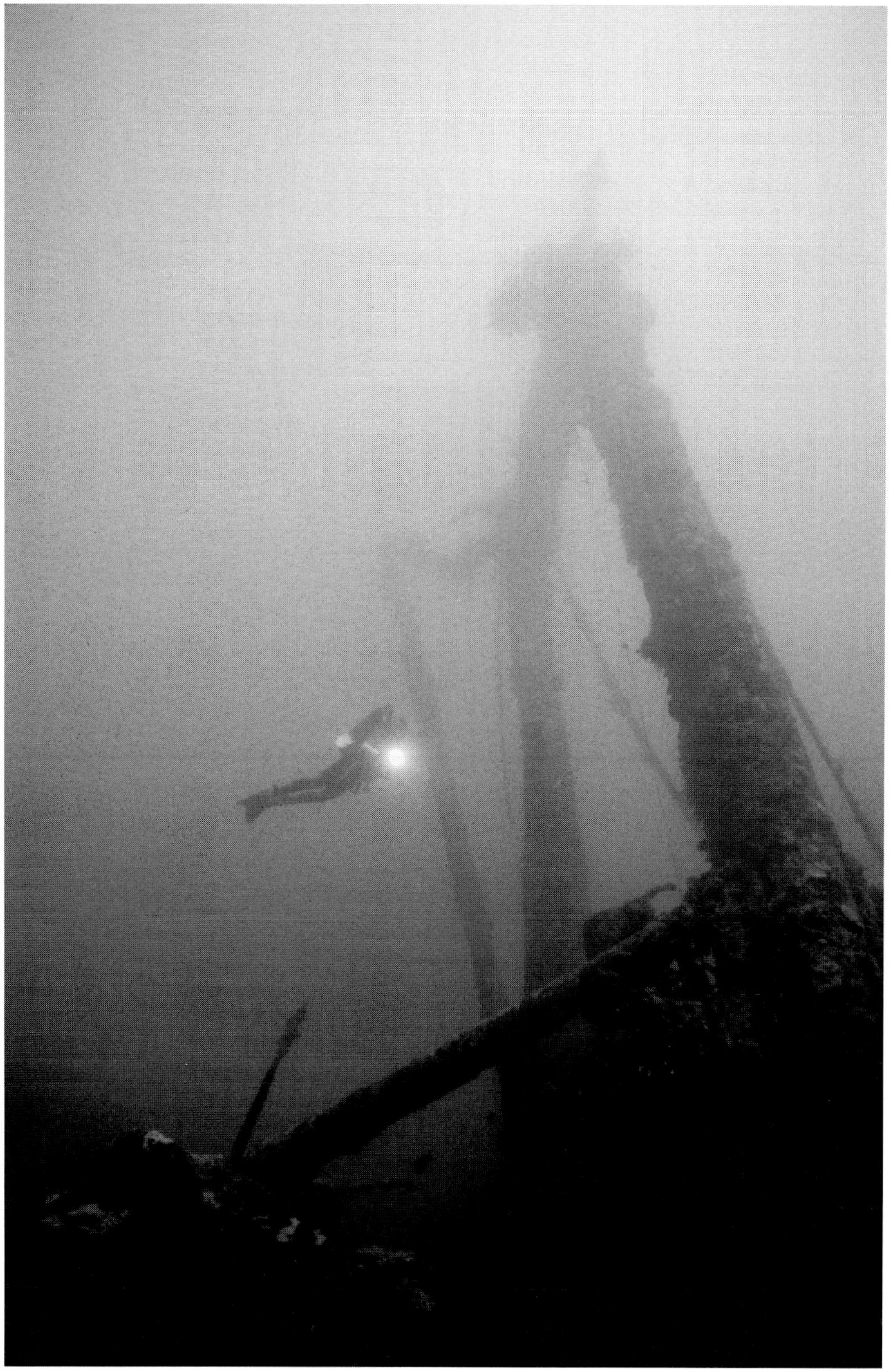

Asakazi Maru, Kwajalein Atoll, Marshall Islands

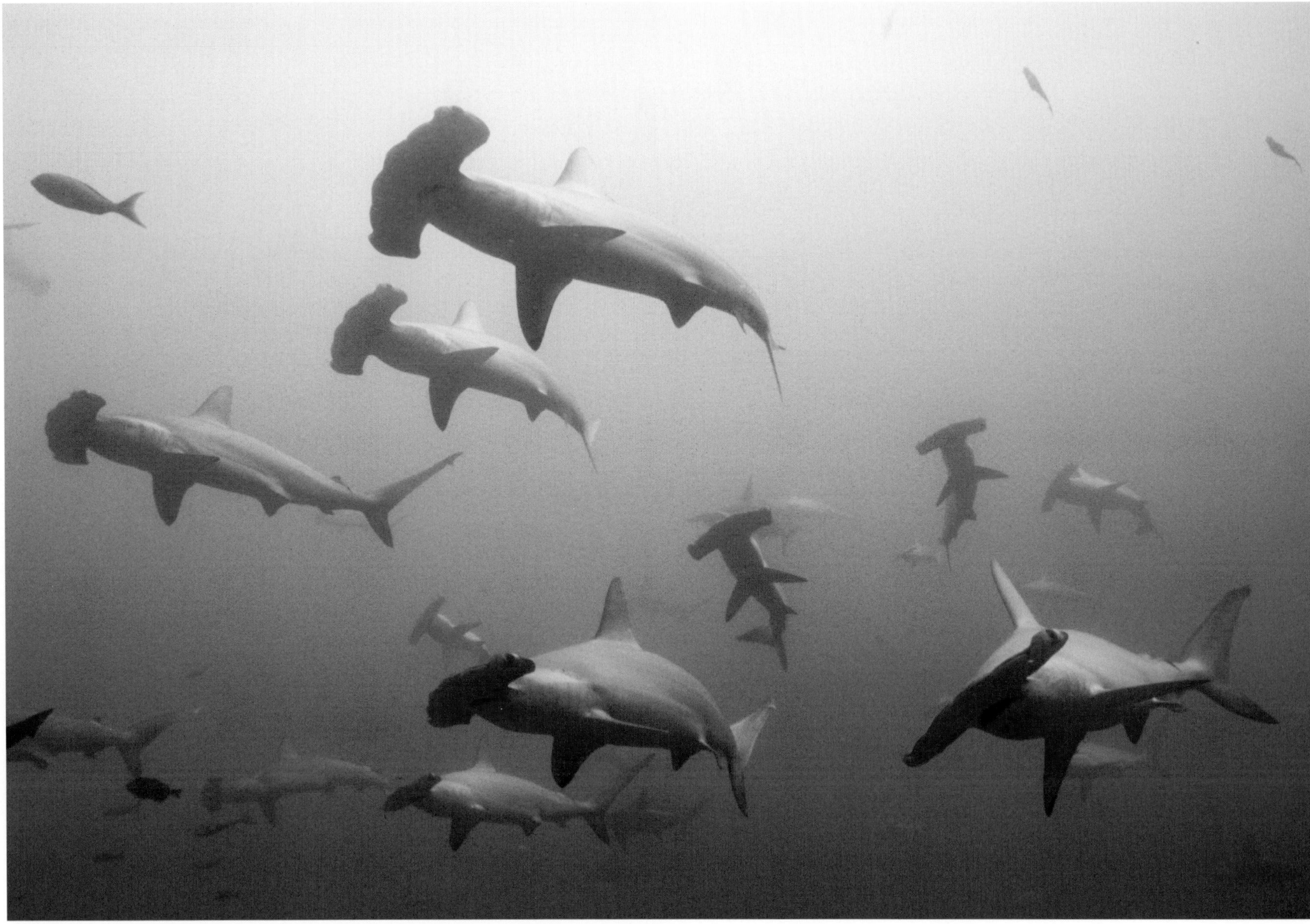

Scalloped Hammerhead sharks, Darwin Island, Galapagos

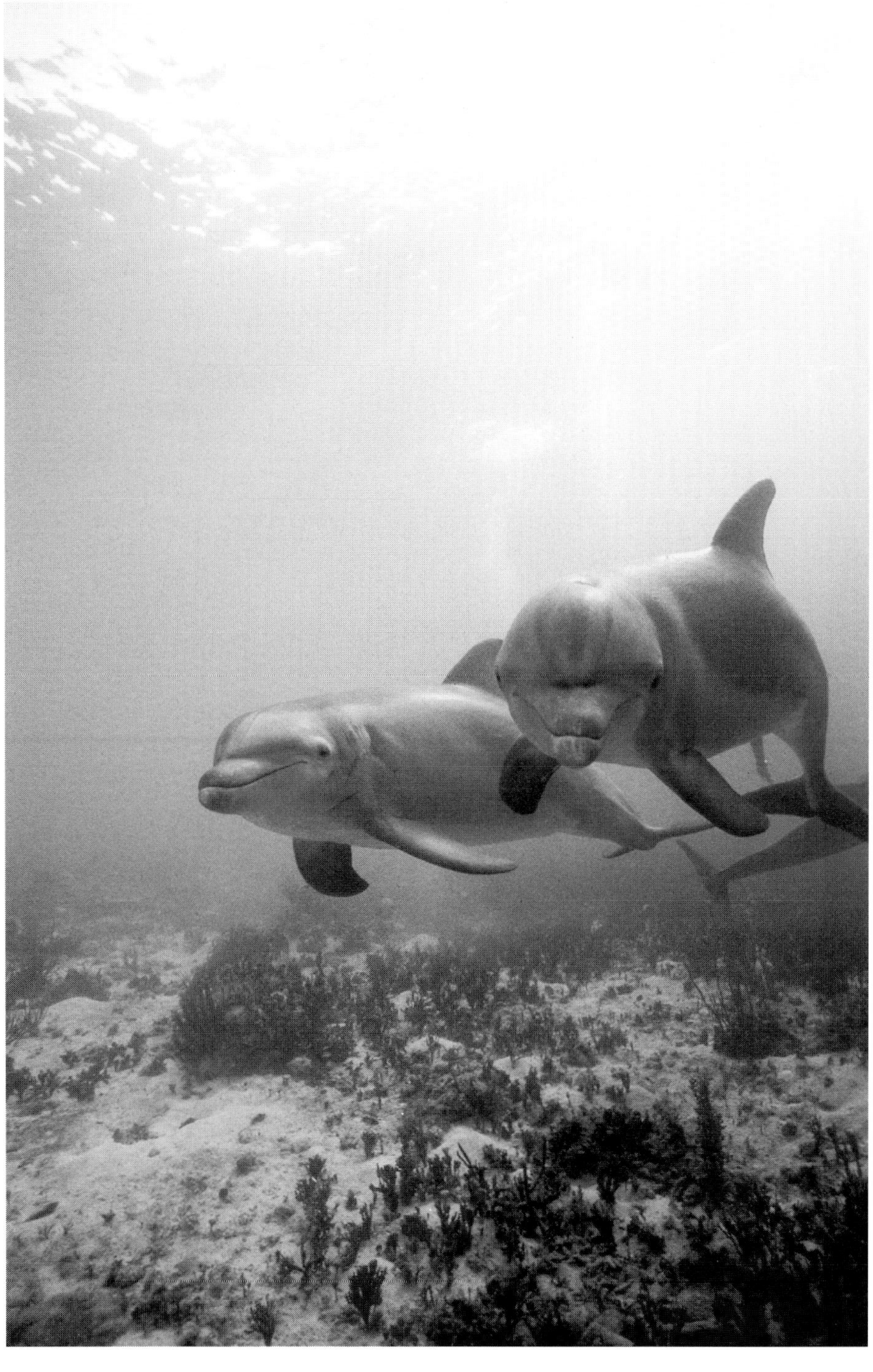

Bottlenosed dolphins, Mexico

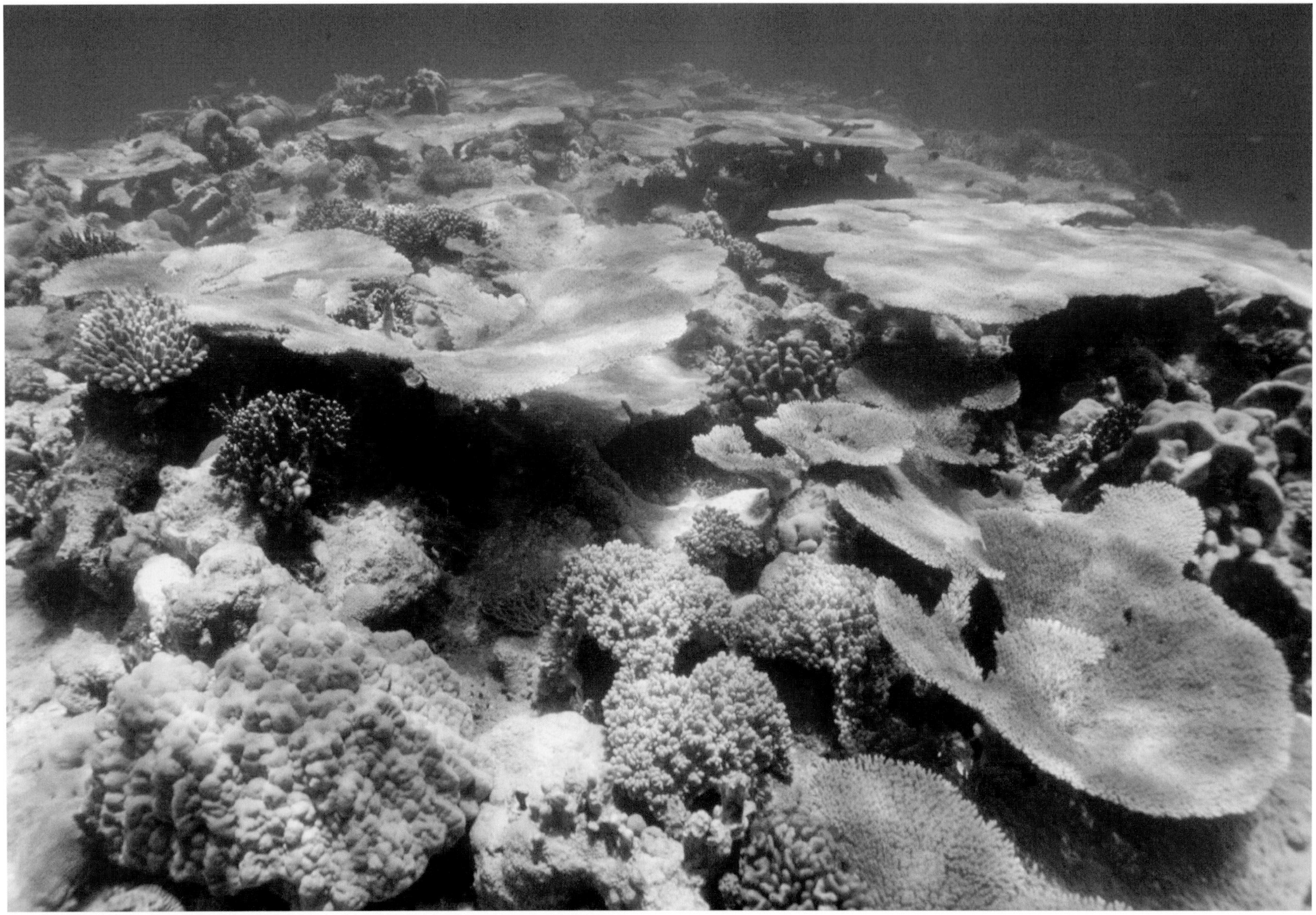

Coral reef, Marshall Islands

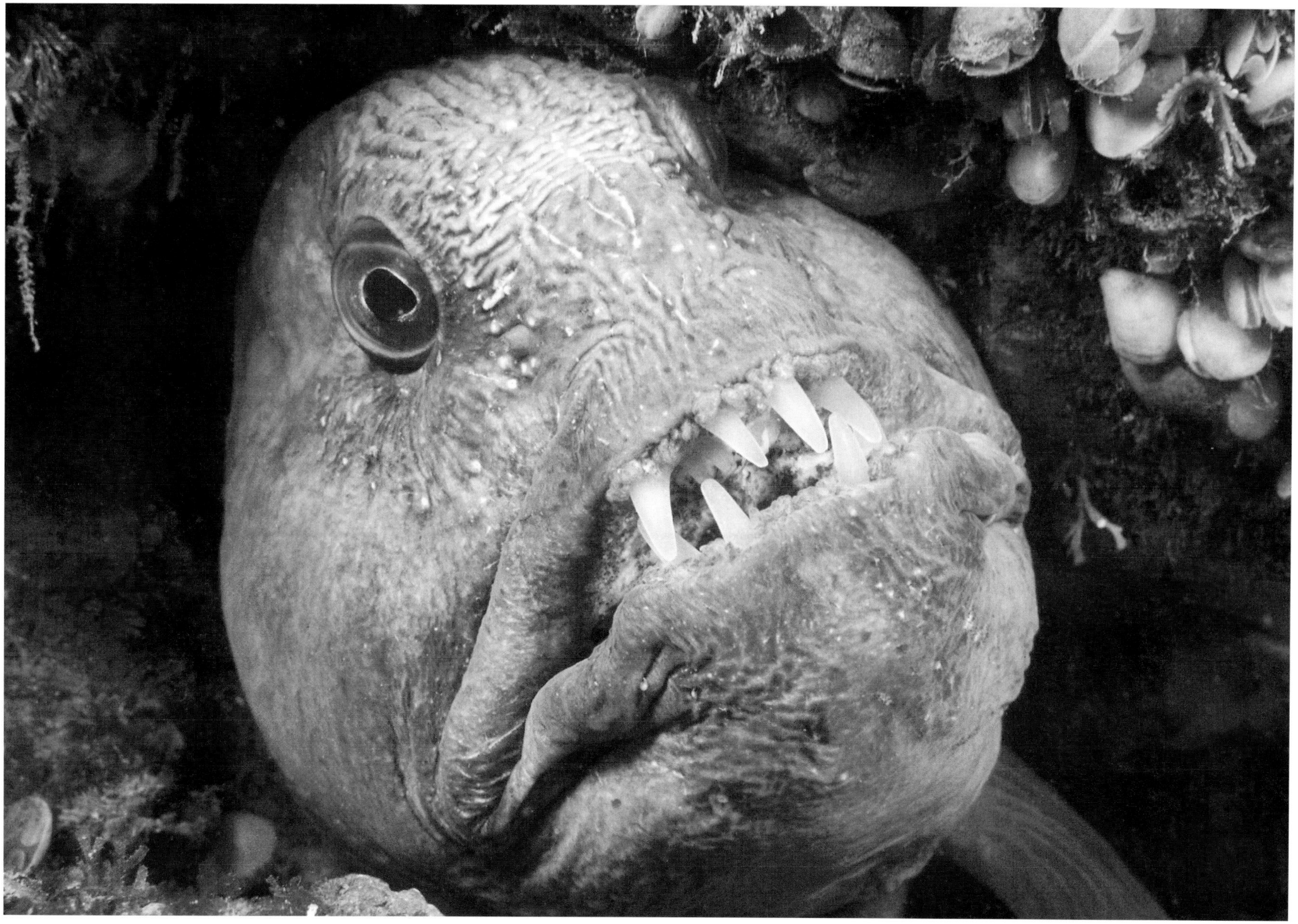

Atlantic Wolffish, Passamaquoddy Bay, Maine

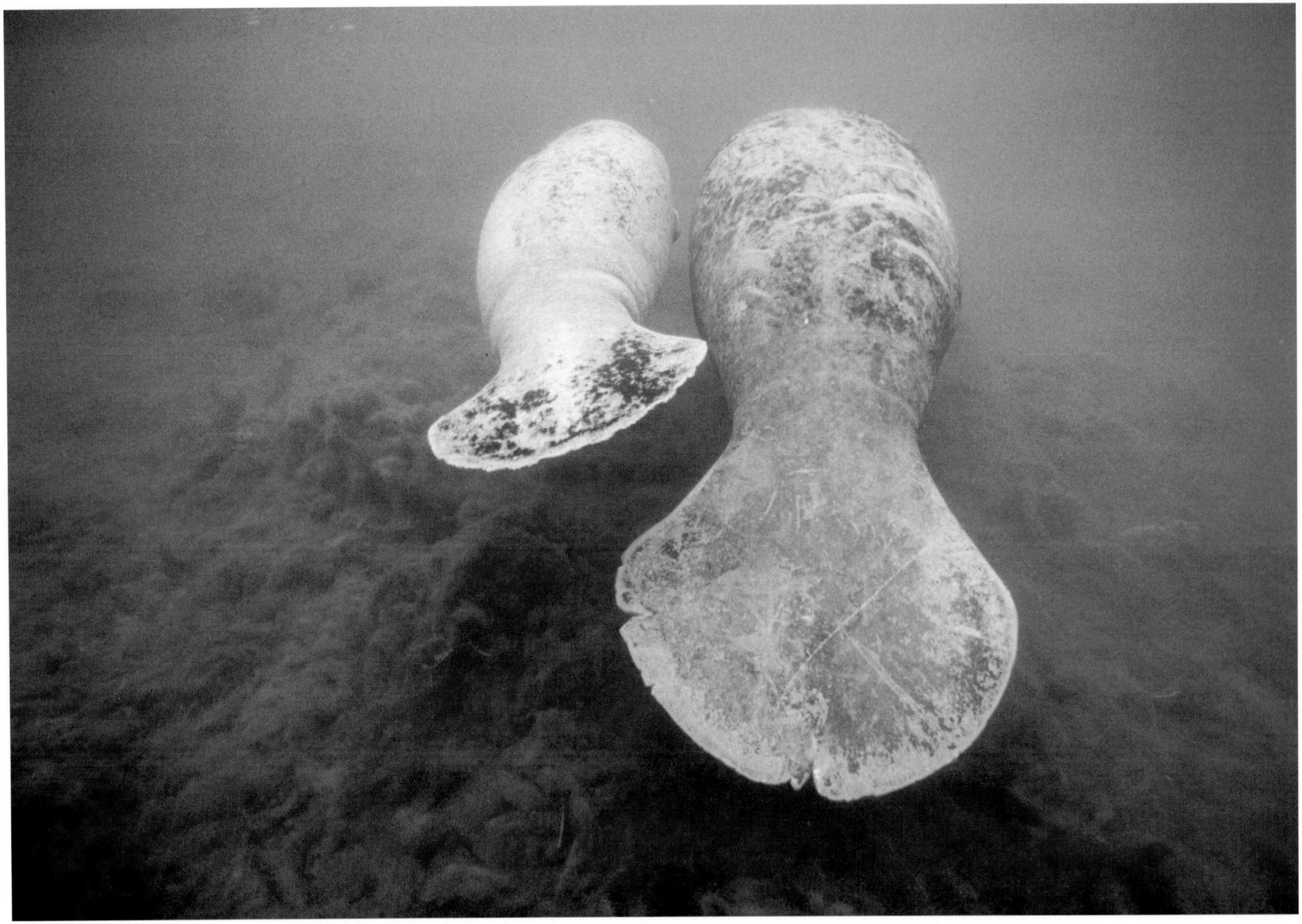

West Indian manatee mother with calf, Crystal River, Florida

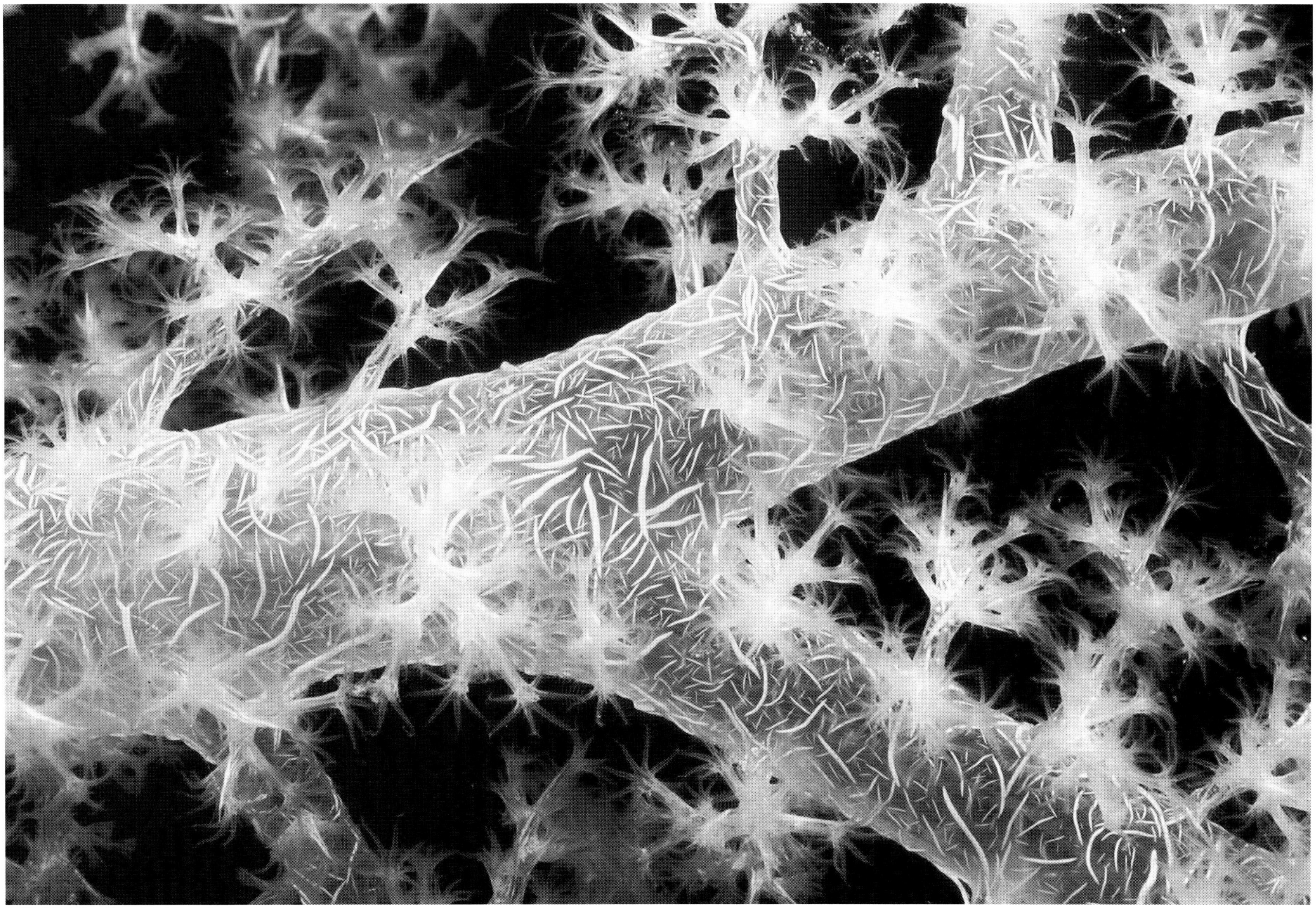

Soft coral, Chuuk Lagoon, Micronesia

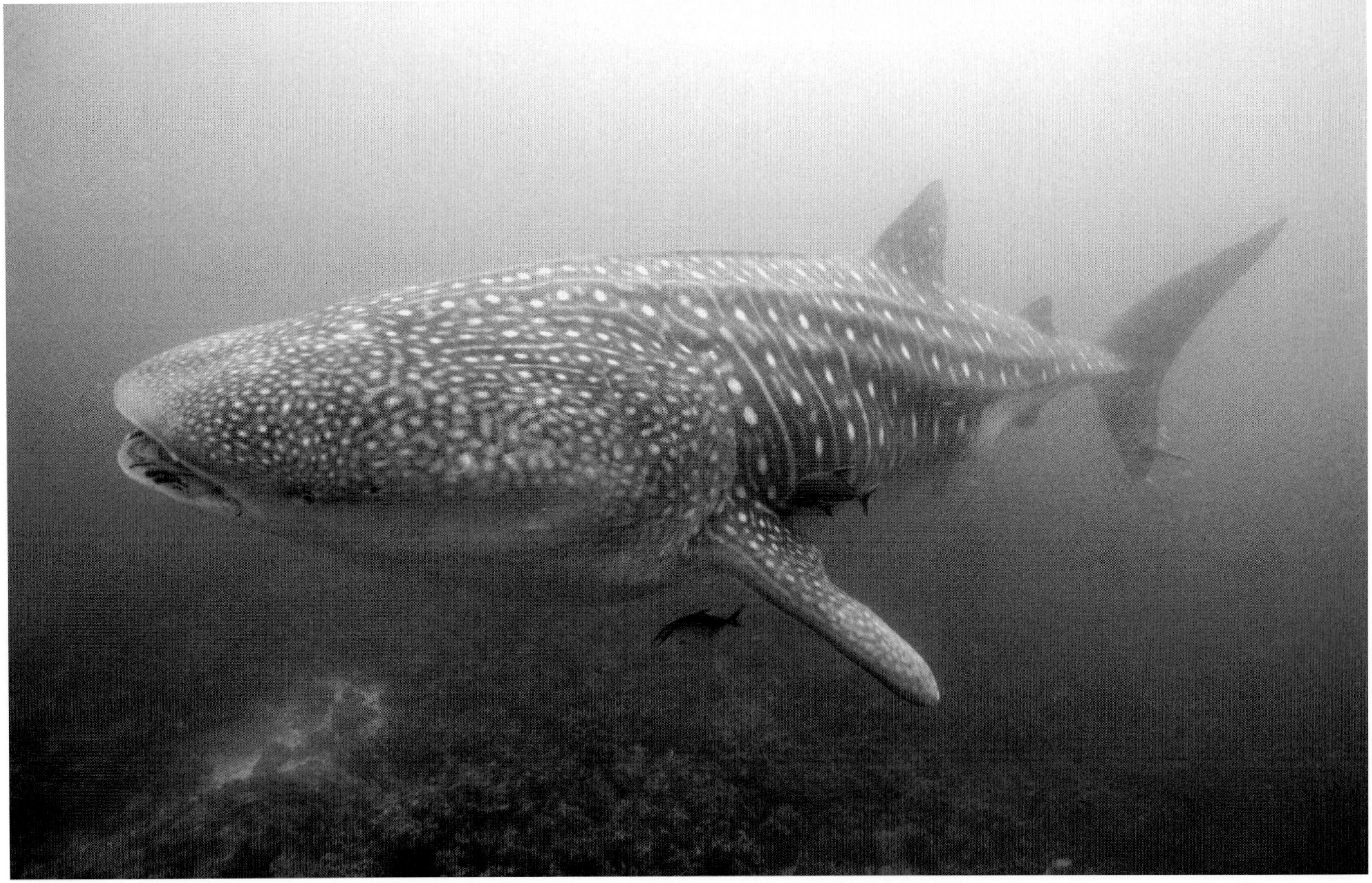

Whale shark, Darwin Island, Galapagos

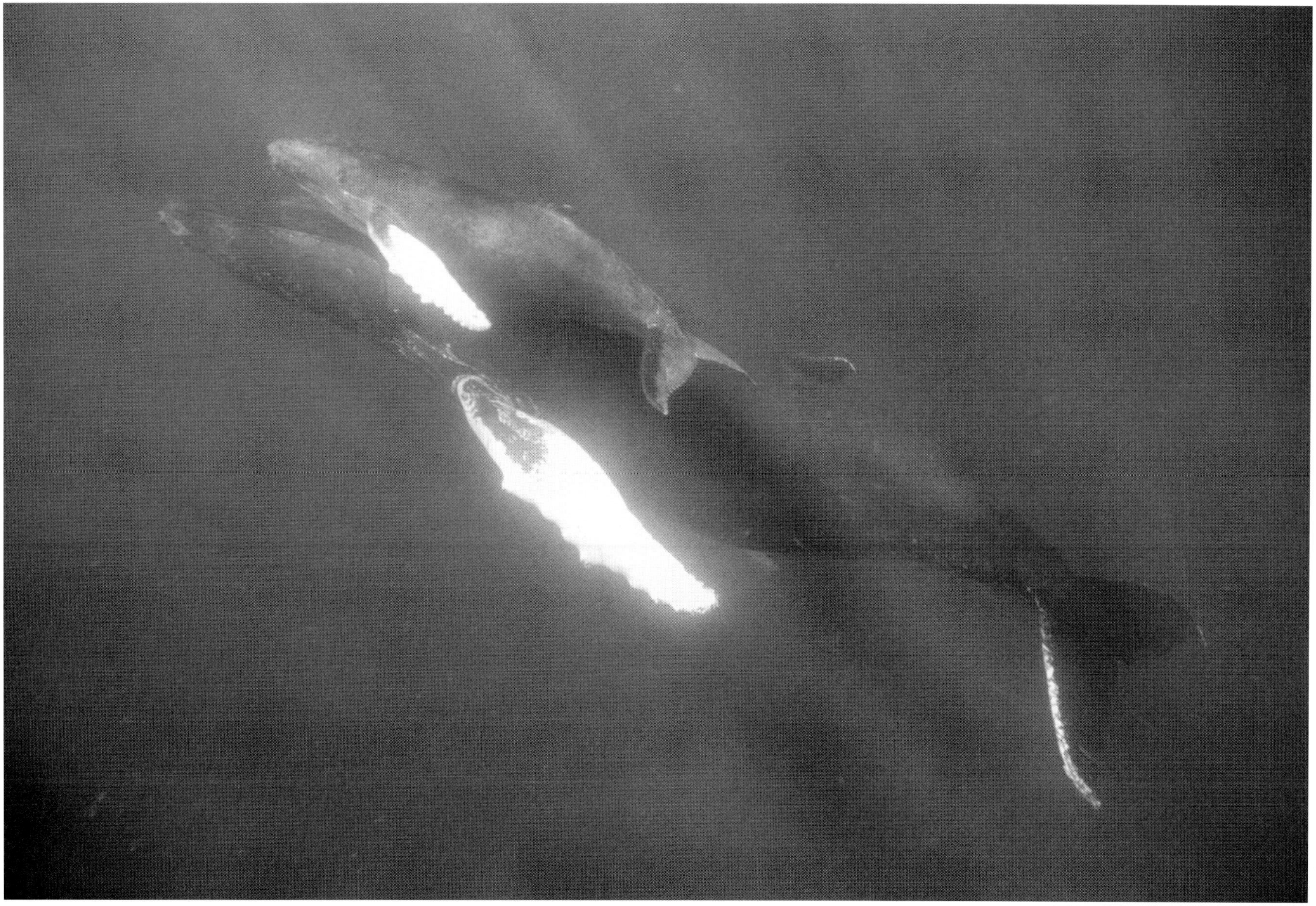

Humpback whale and calf, Silver Banks, Dominican Republic

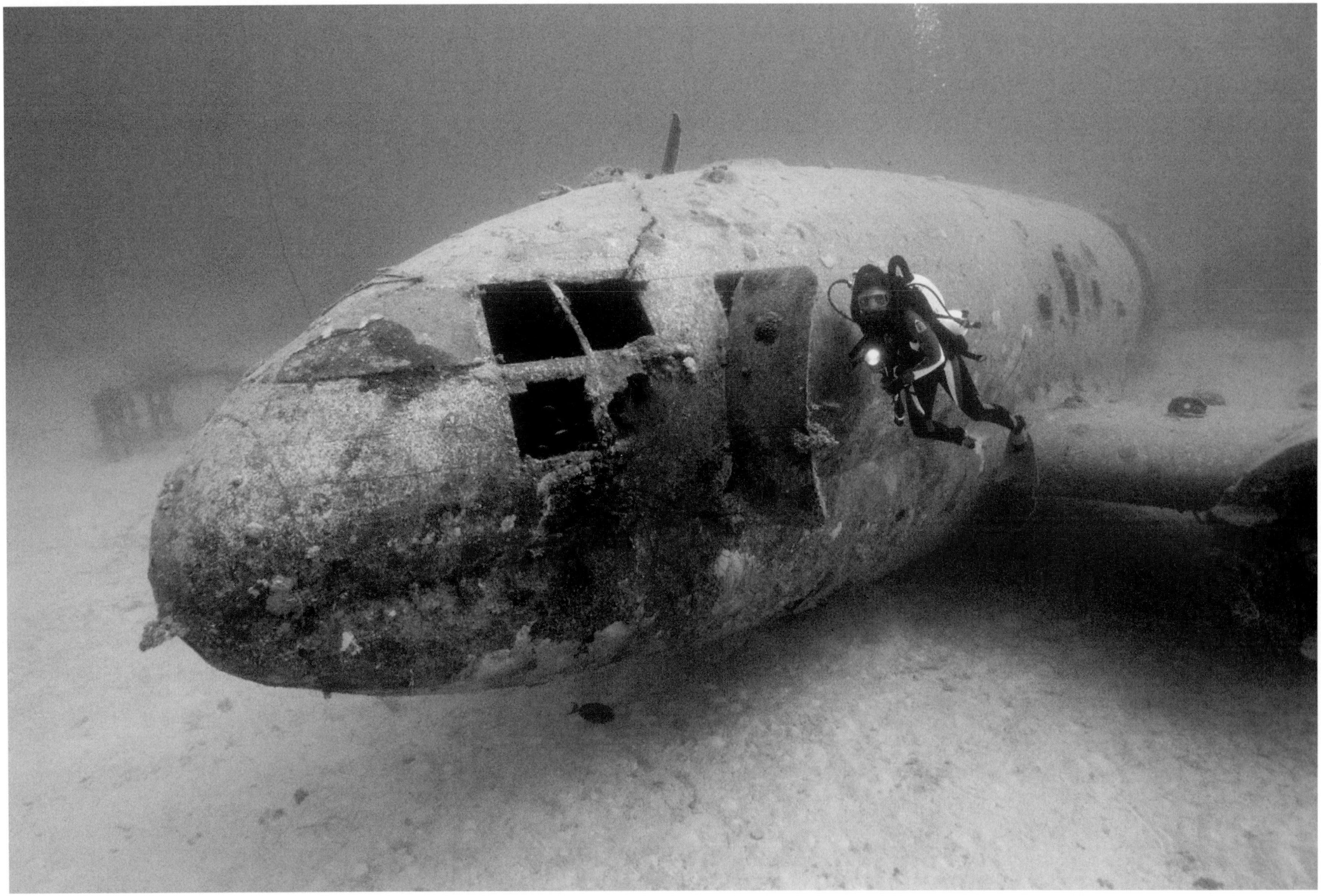

C-46 aircraft, Kwajalein Atoll, Marshall Islands

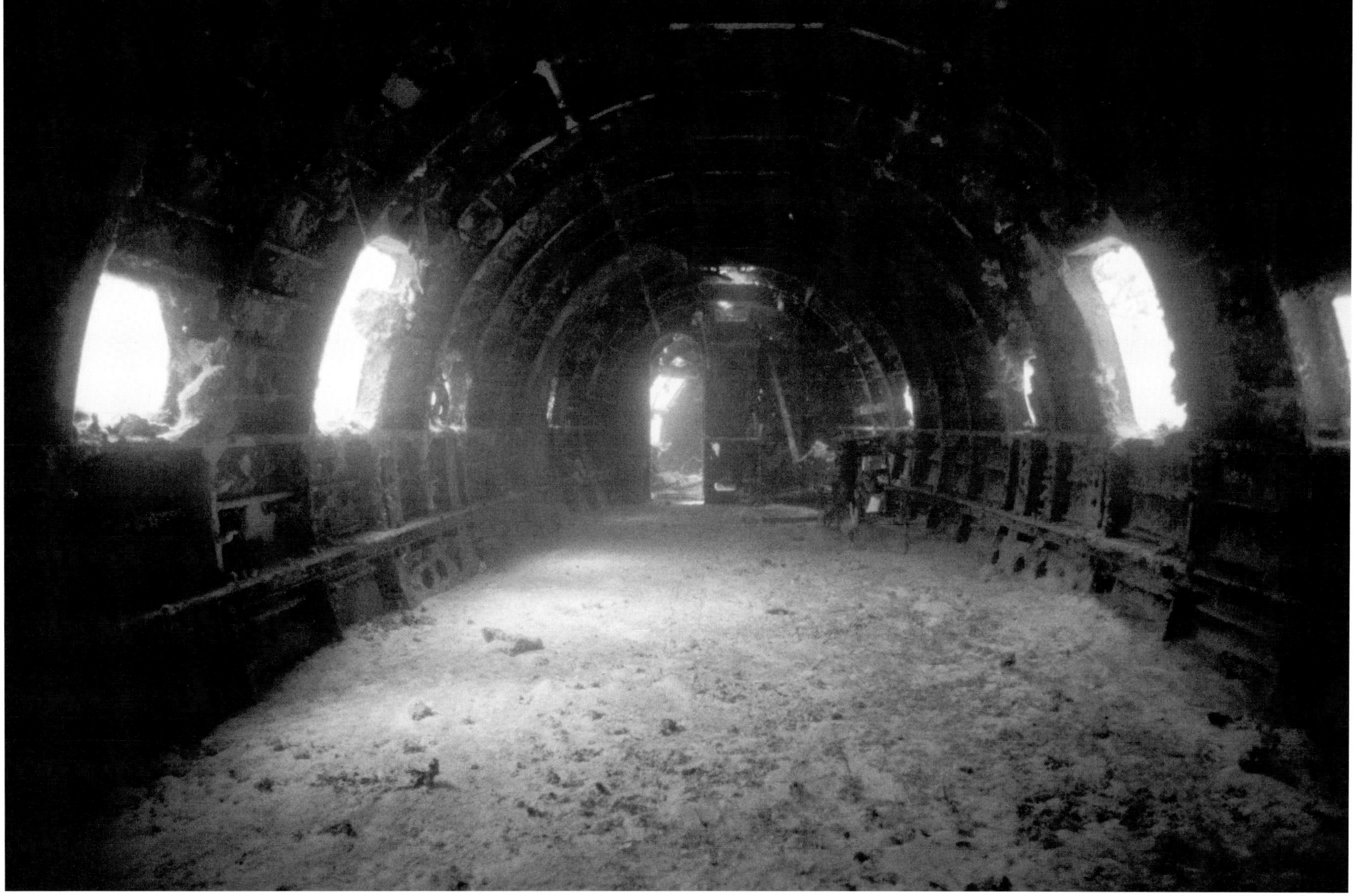

C-46 aircraft interior, Kwajalein Atoll, Marshall Islands

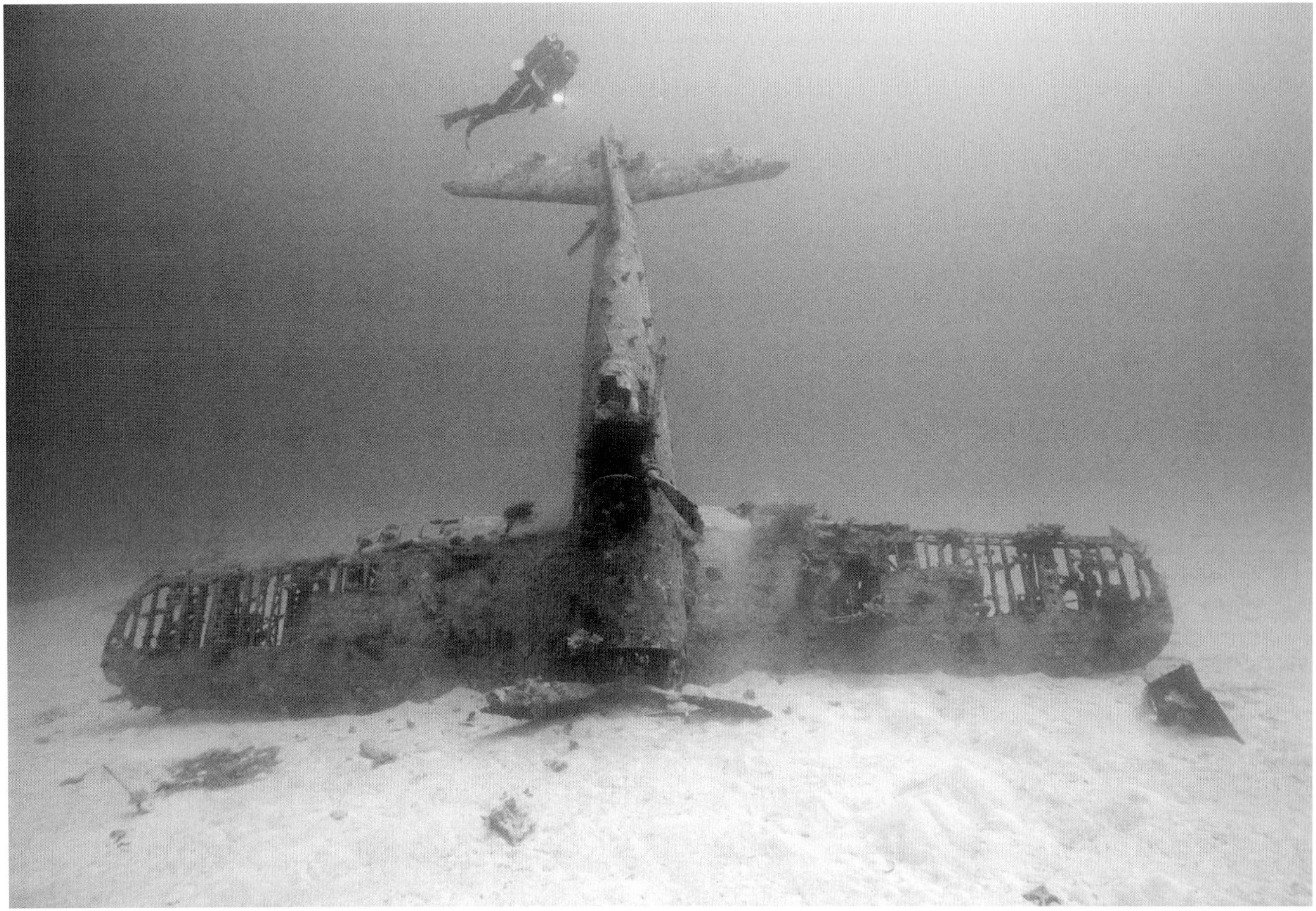

F4U Corsair aircraft, Kwajalein Atoll, Marshall Islands

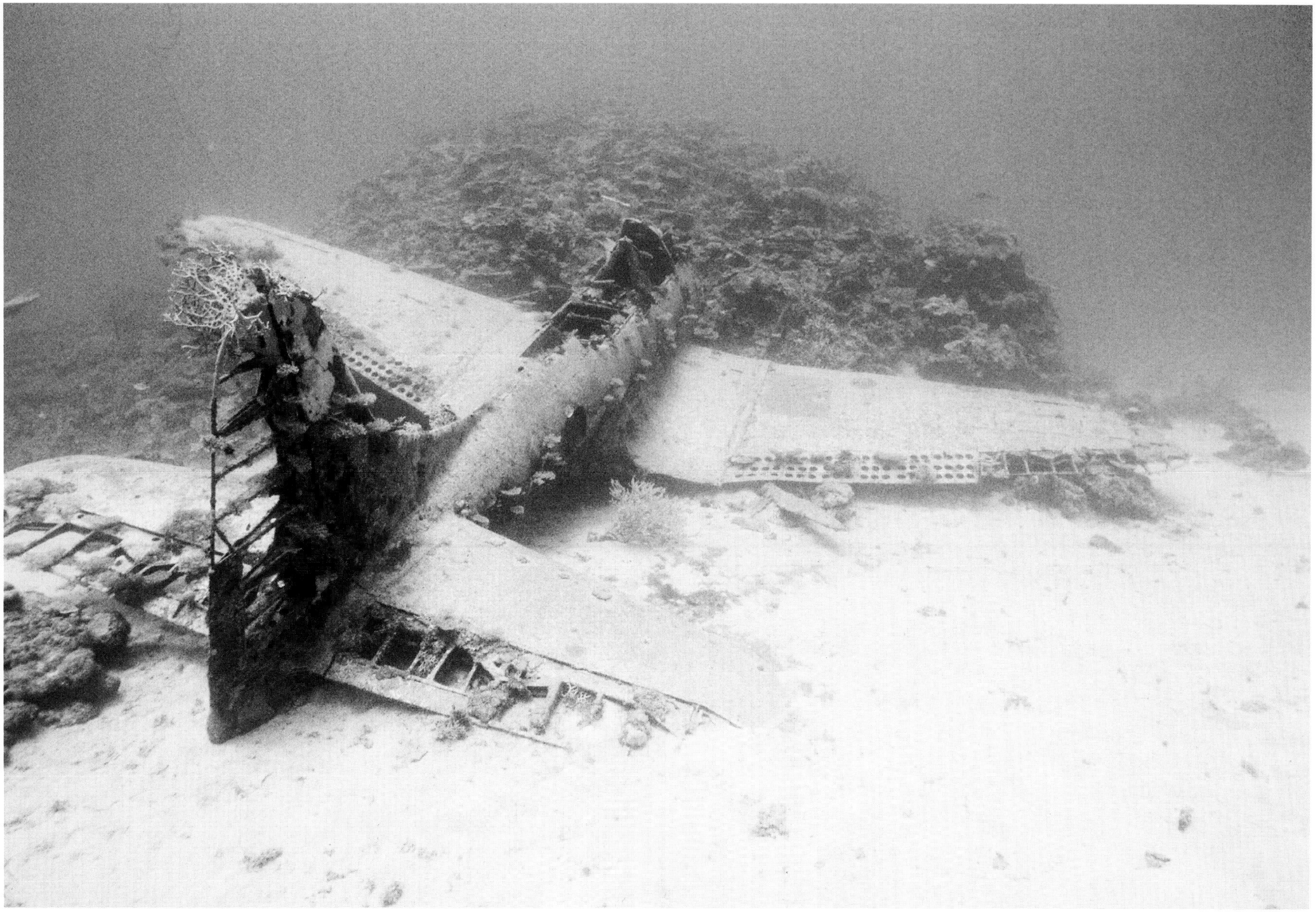

Dauntless SBD aircraft, Kwajalein Atoll, Marshall Islands

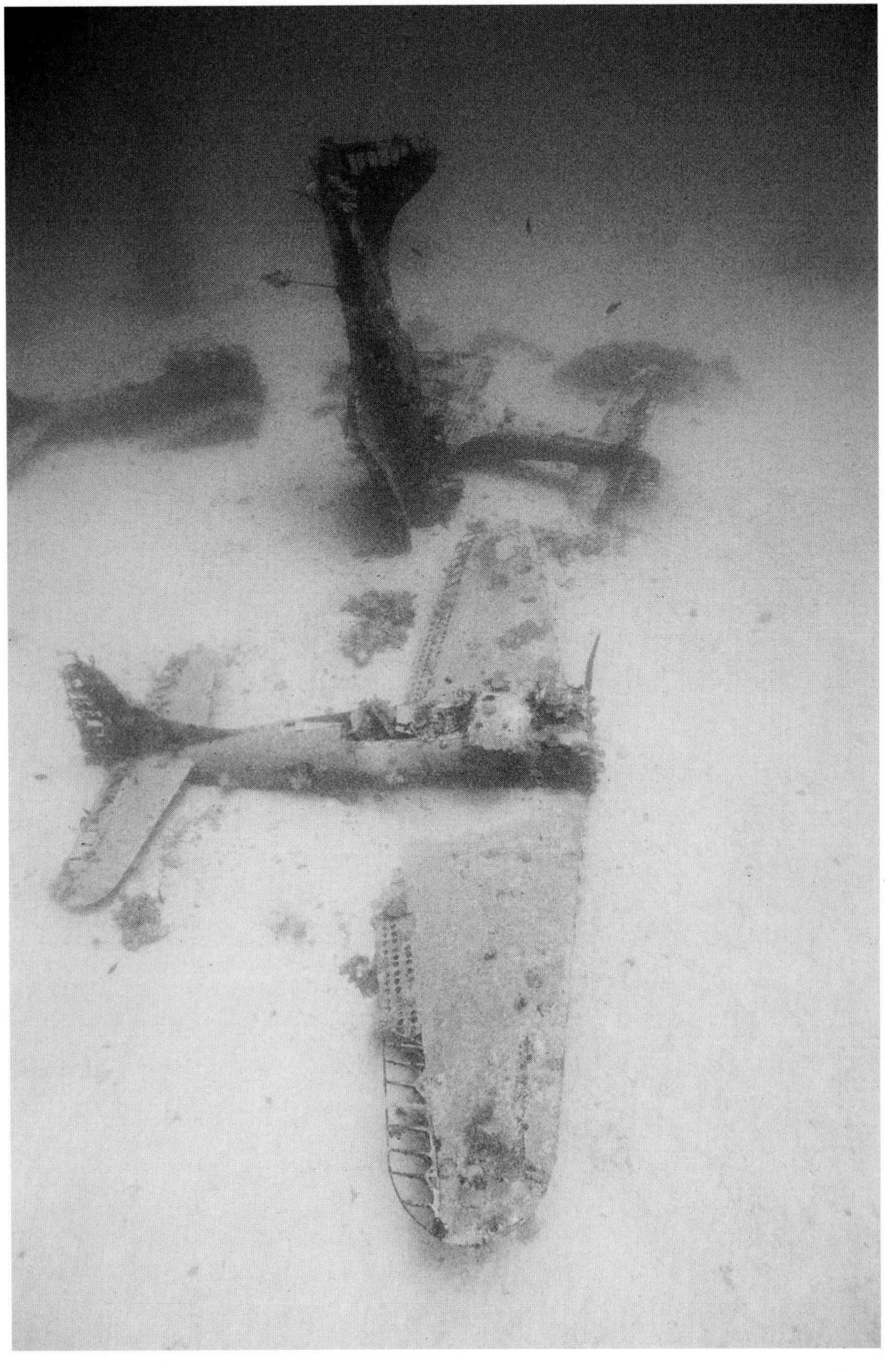

Dauntless SBD aircraft, Kwajalein Atoll, Marshall Islands

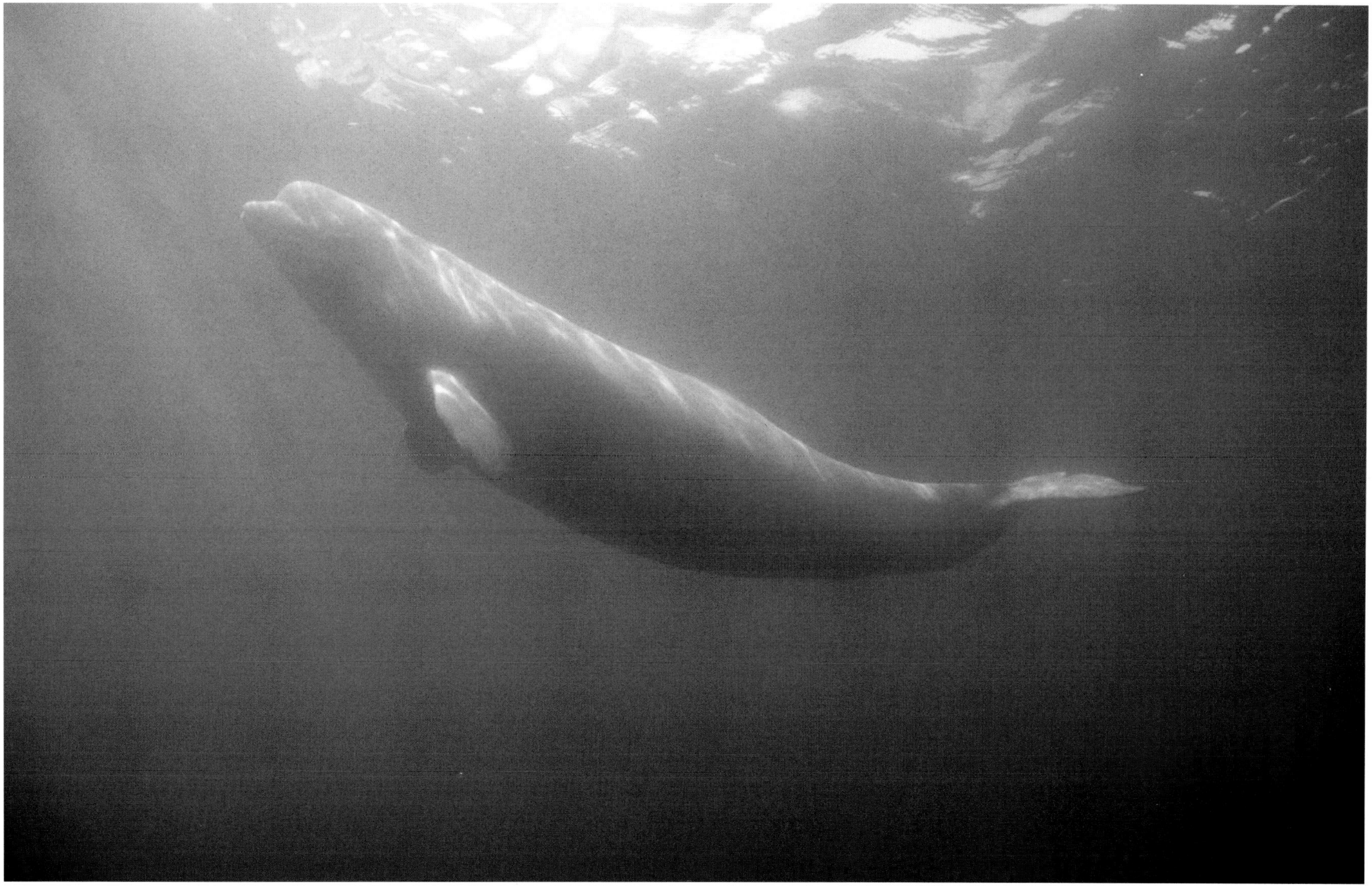

Beluga whale, Canada

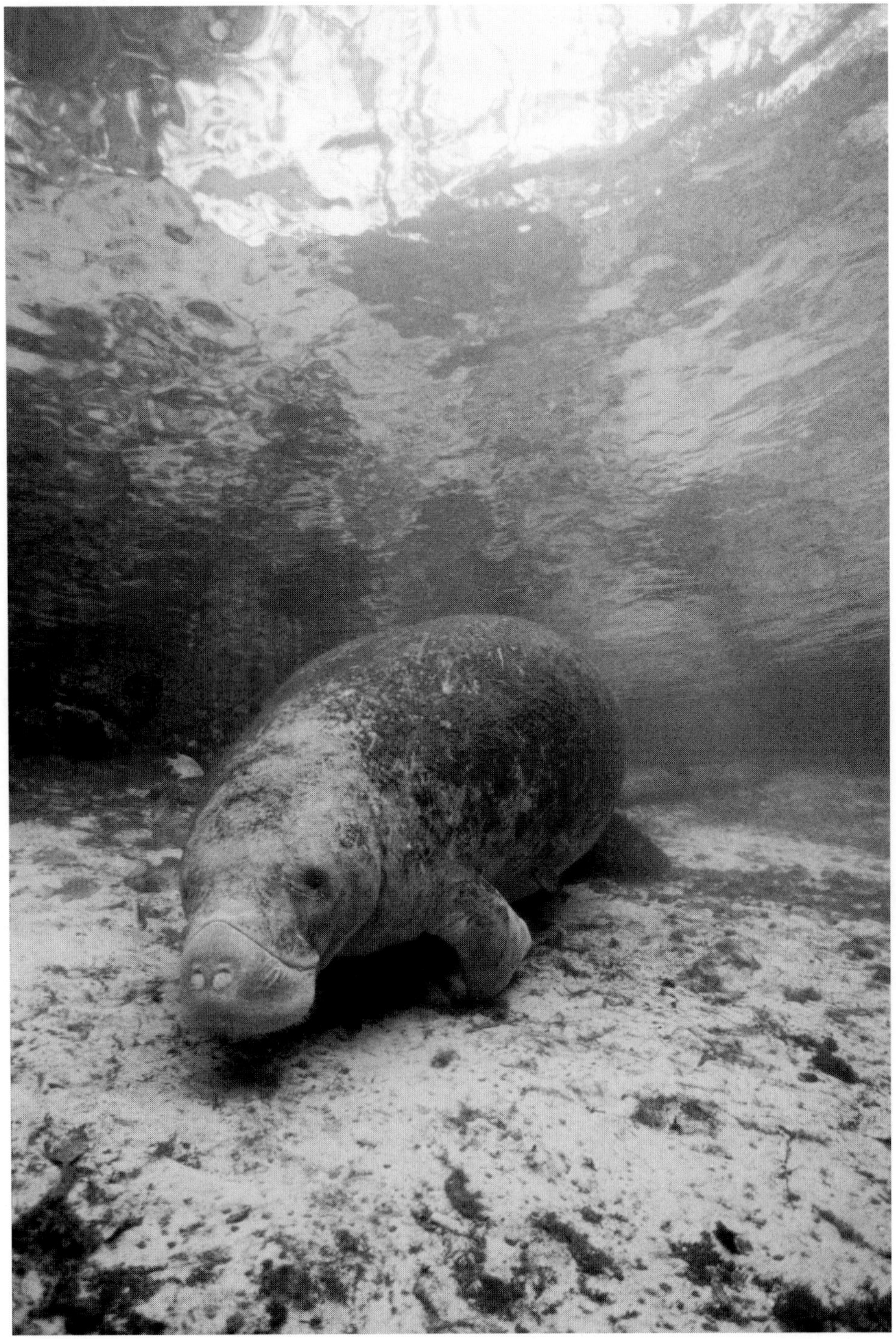

West Indian manatee, Crystal River, Florida

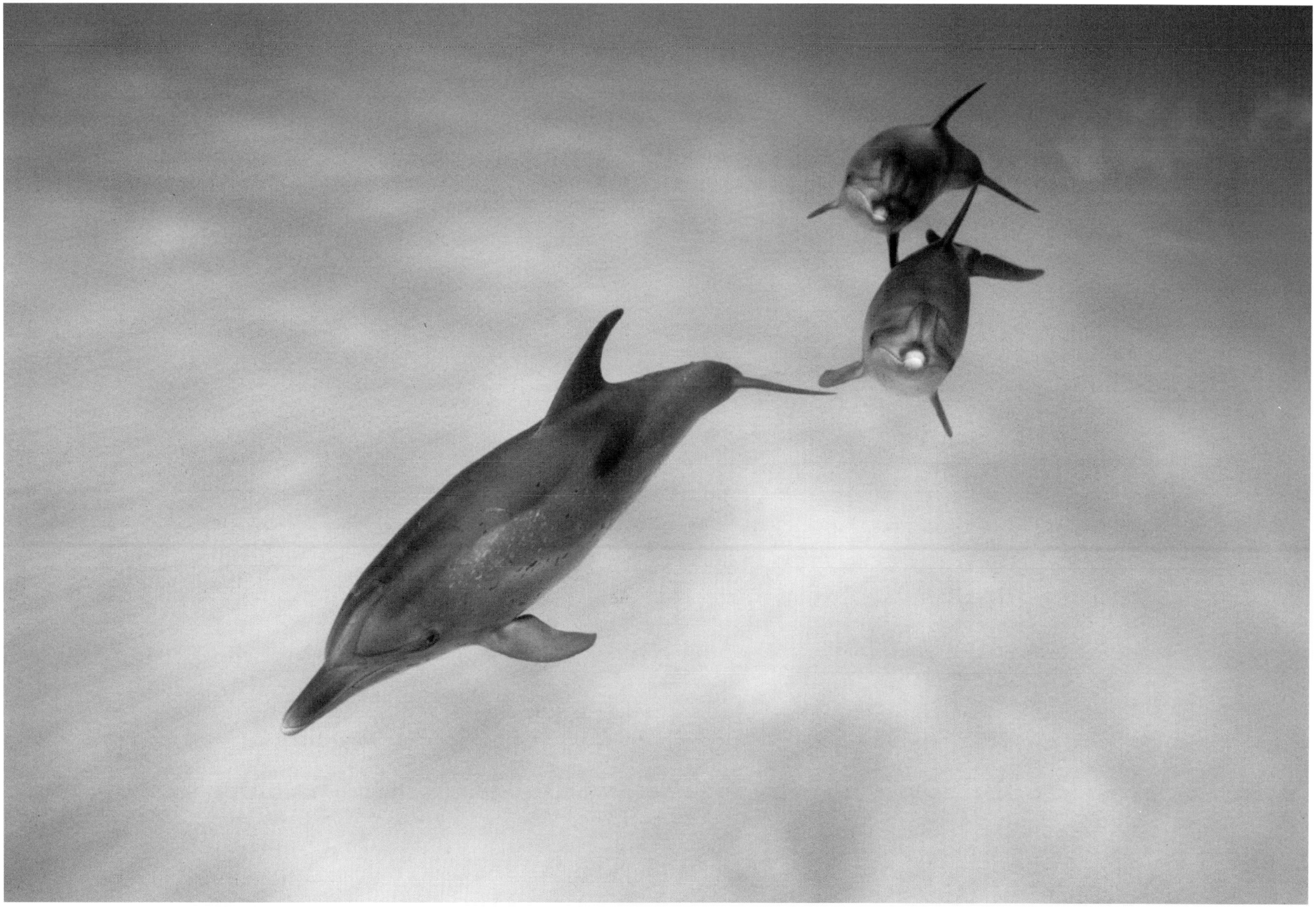

Spotted dolphins, Little Bahama Banks, Bahamas

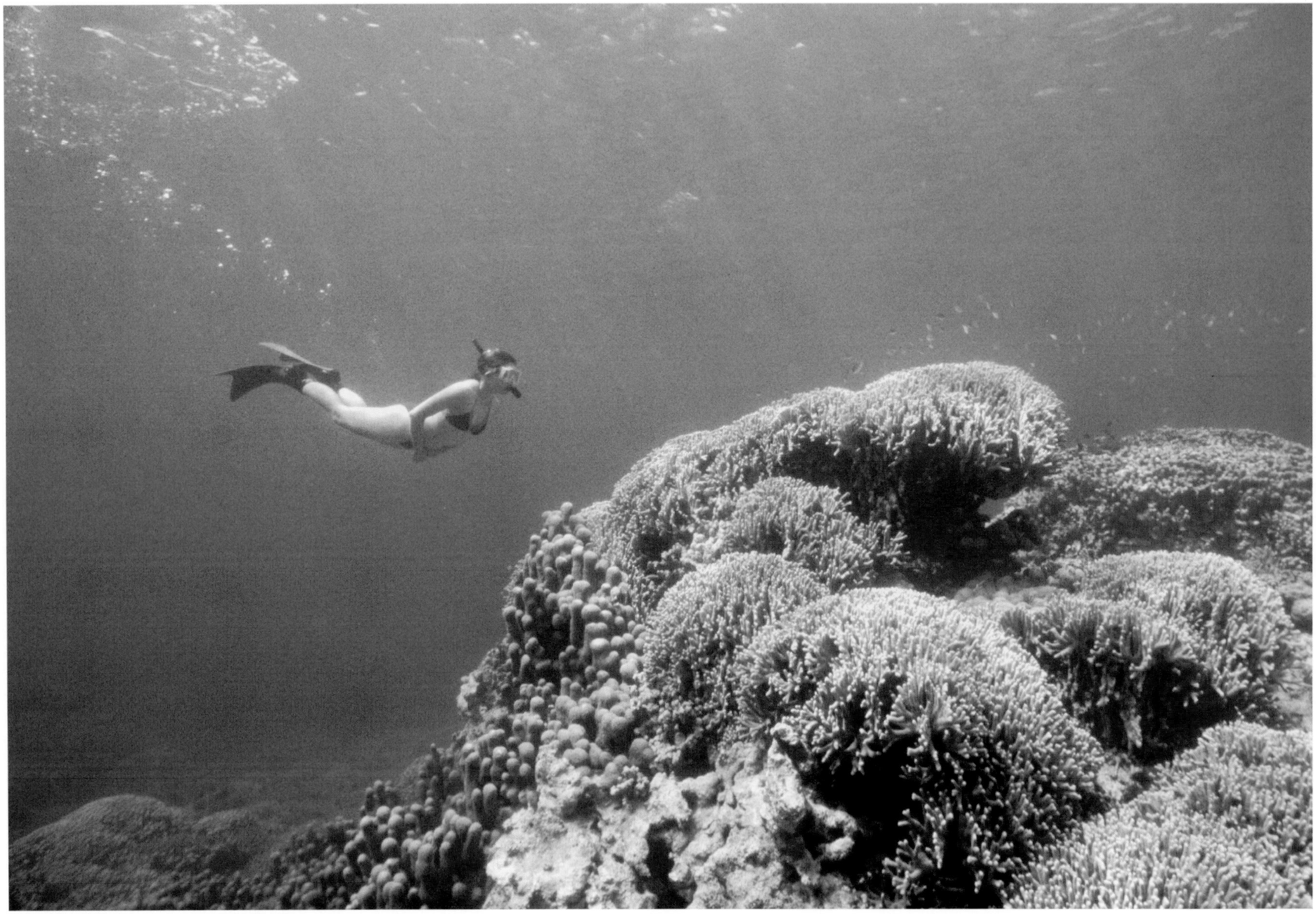

Coral reef, Marshall Islands

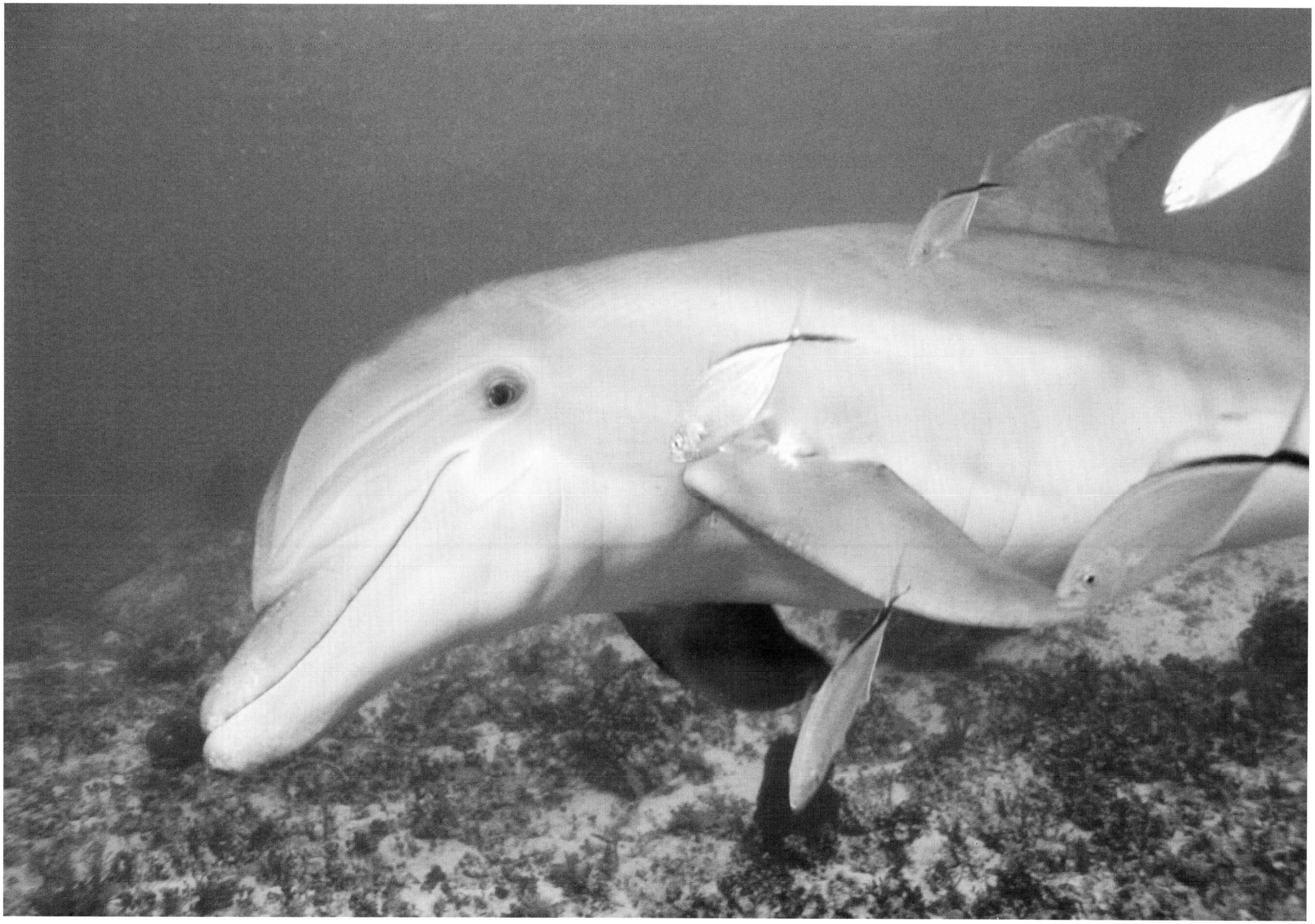

Bottlenosed dolphin, Mexico

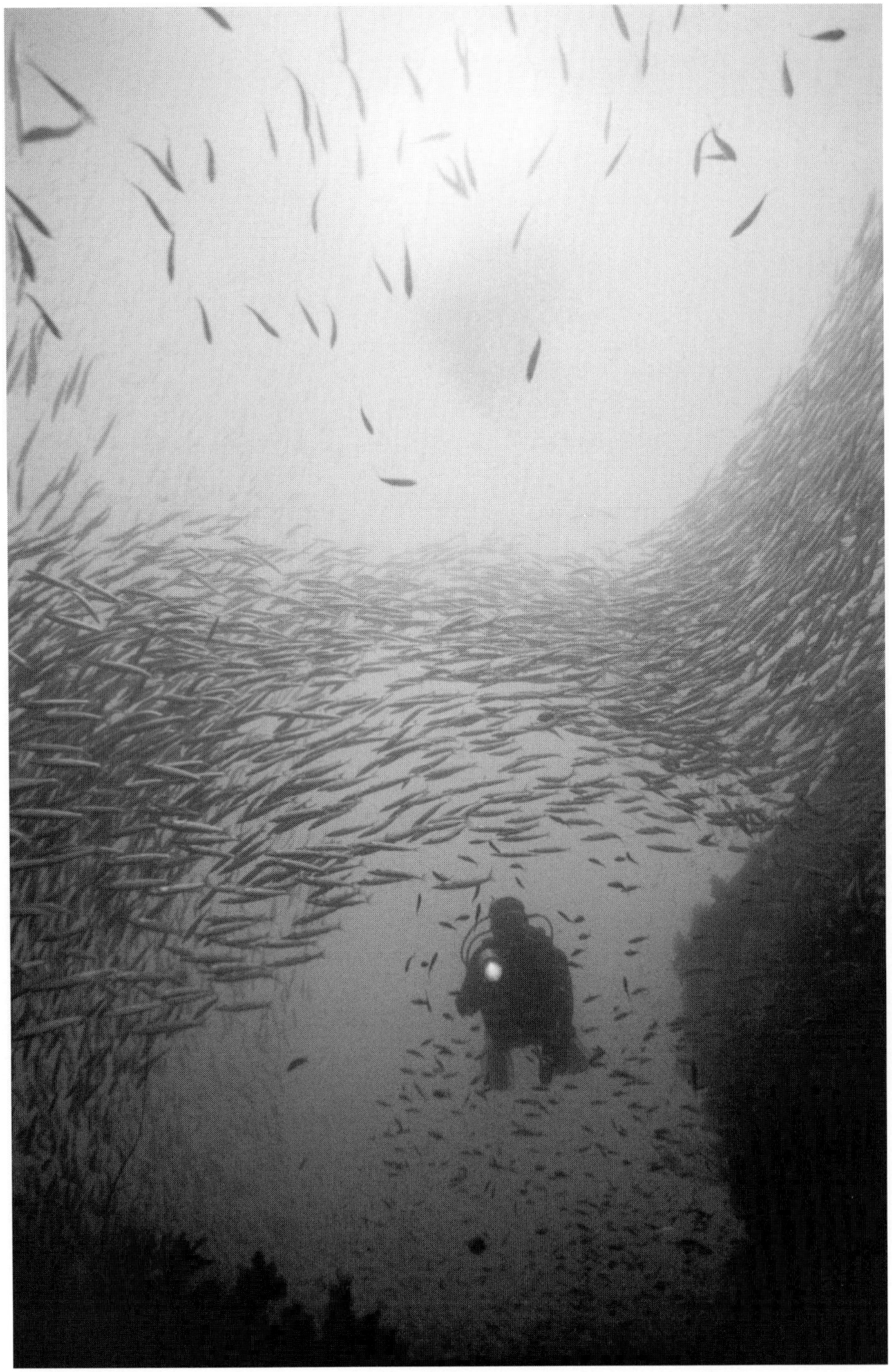

Diver and school of fish, Labuan, Malaysia

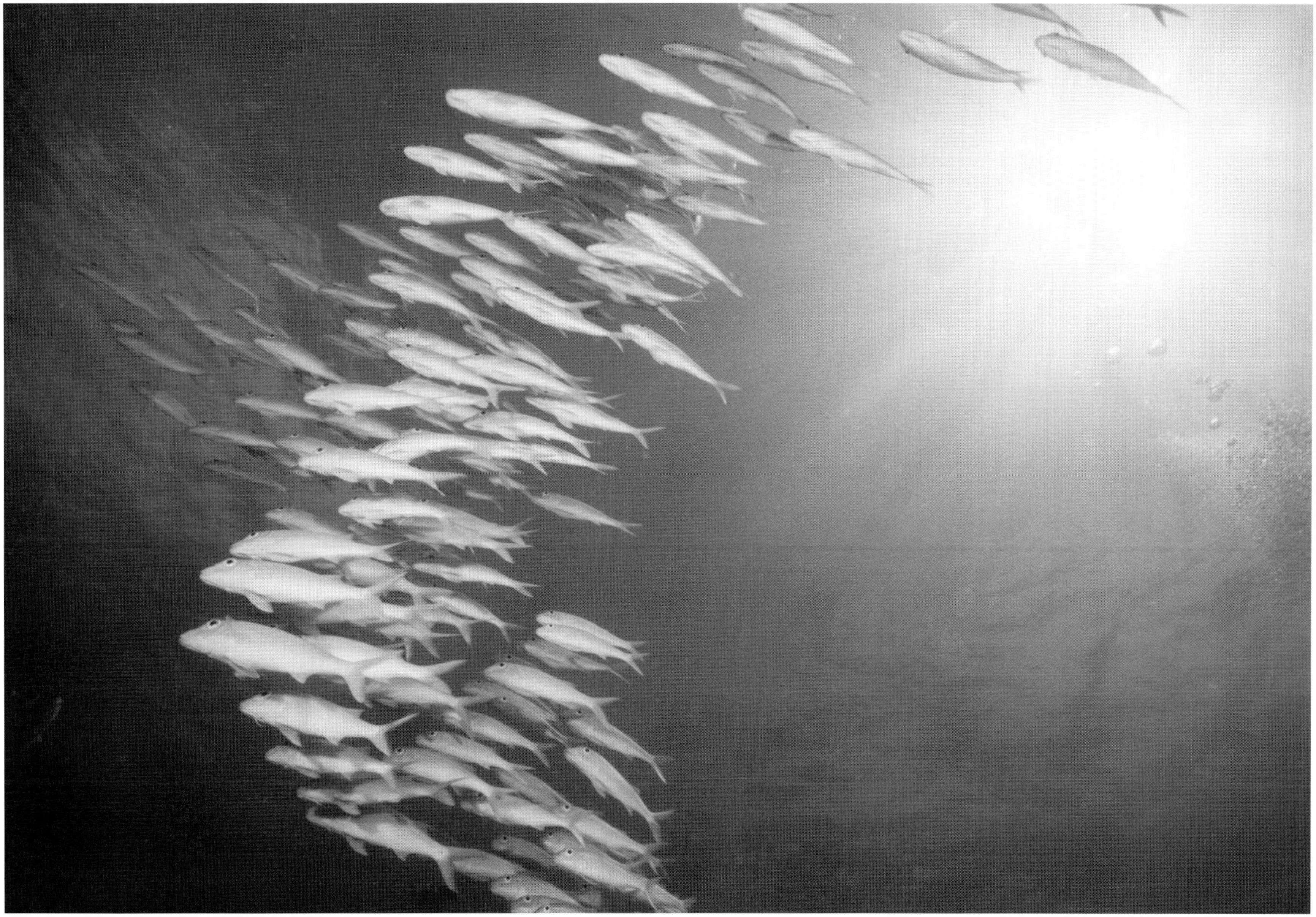

Goatfish, Midway Atoll

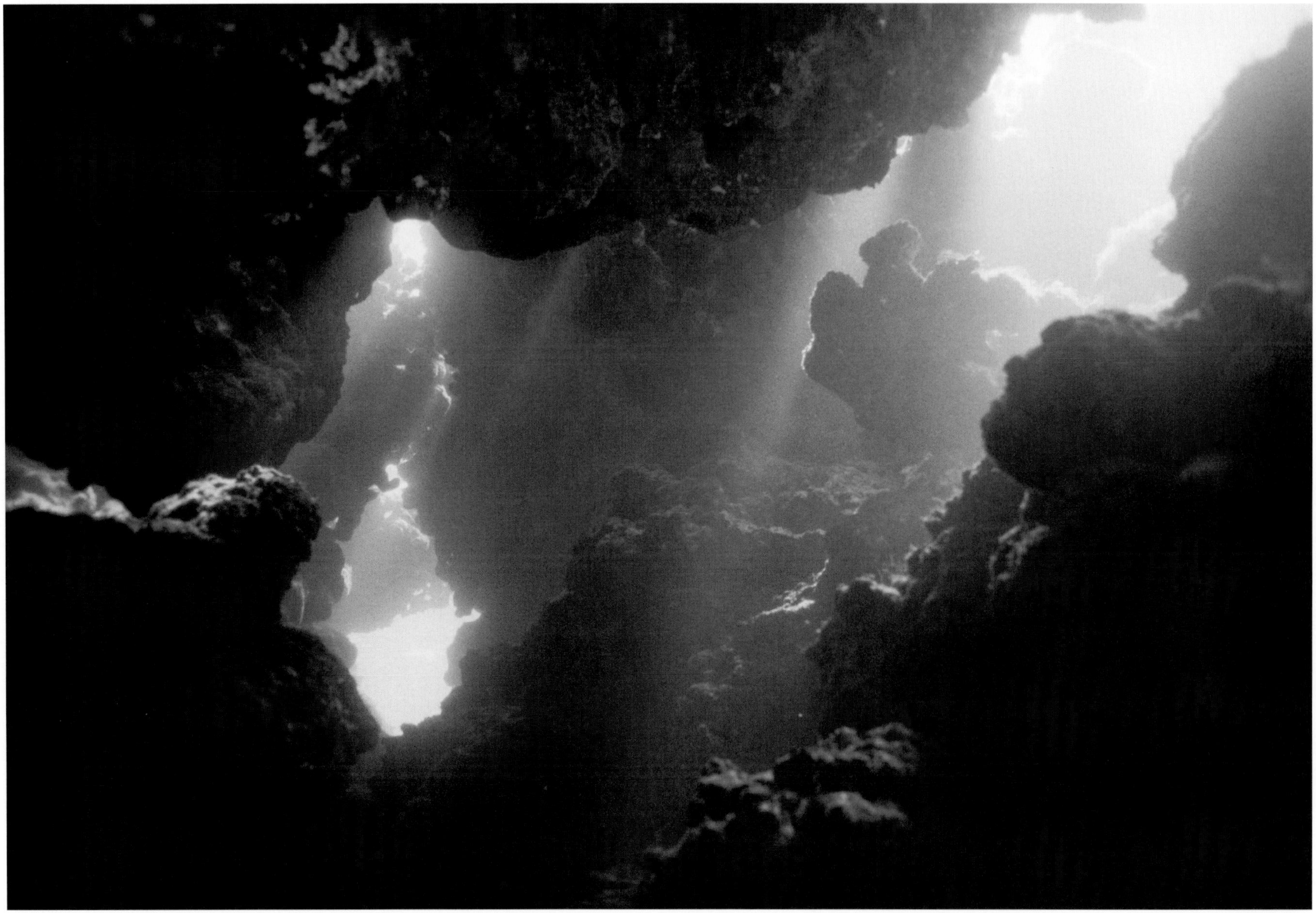

Coral cavern, Bahamas

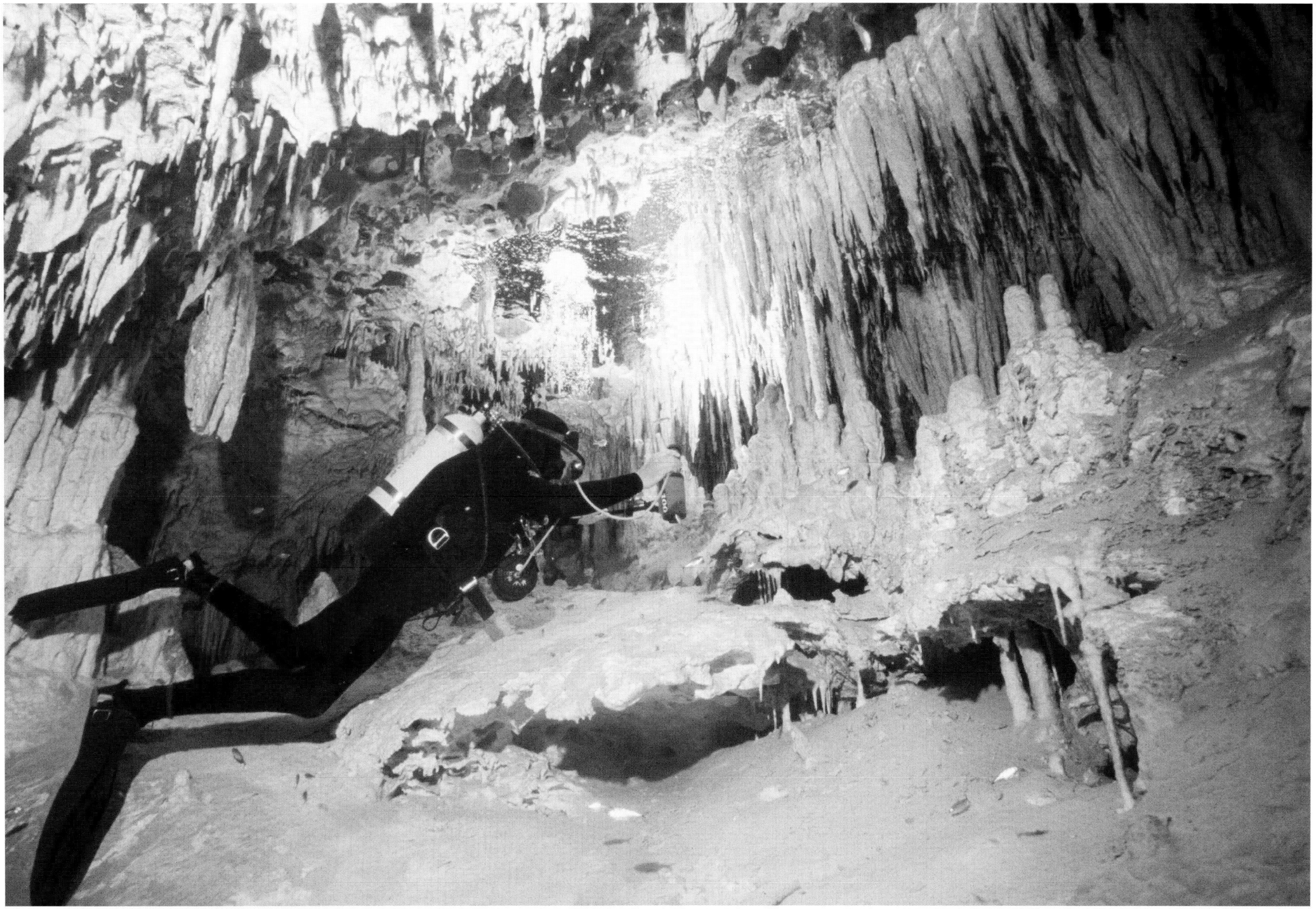

Diver in Dos Ojos cenote, Yucatan, Mexico

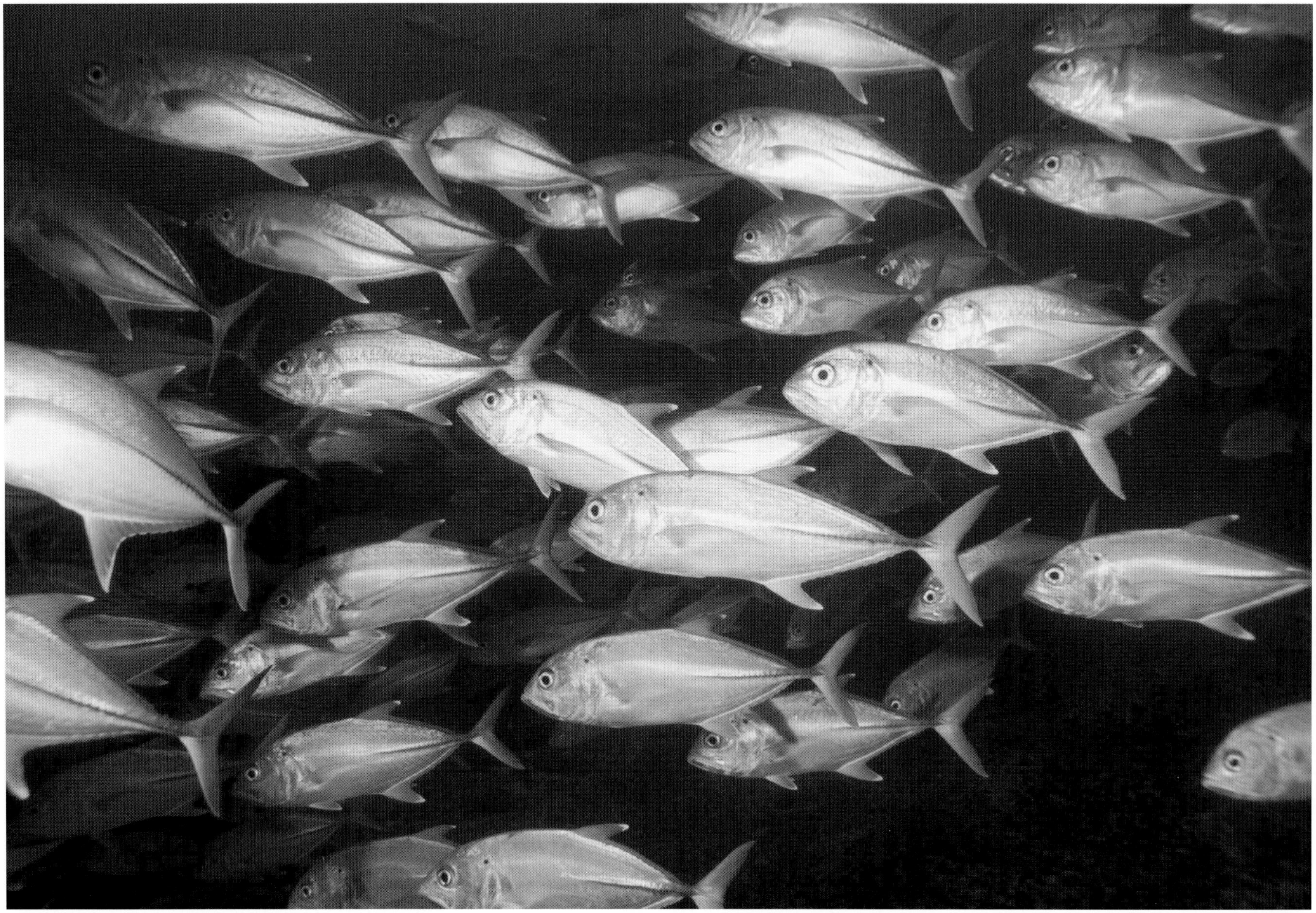

School of jacks, Fiji

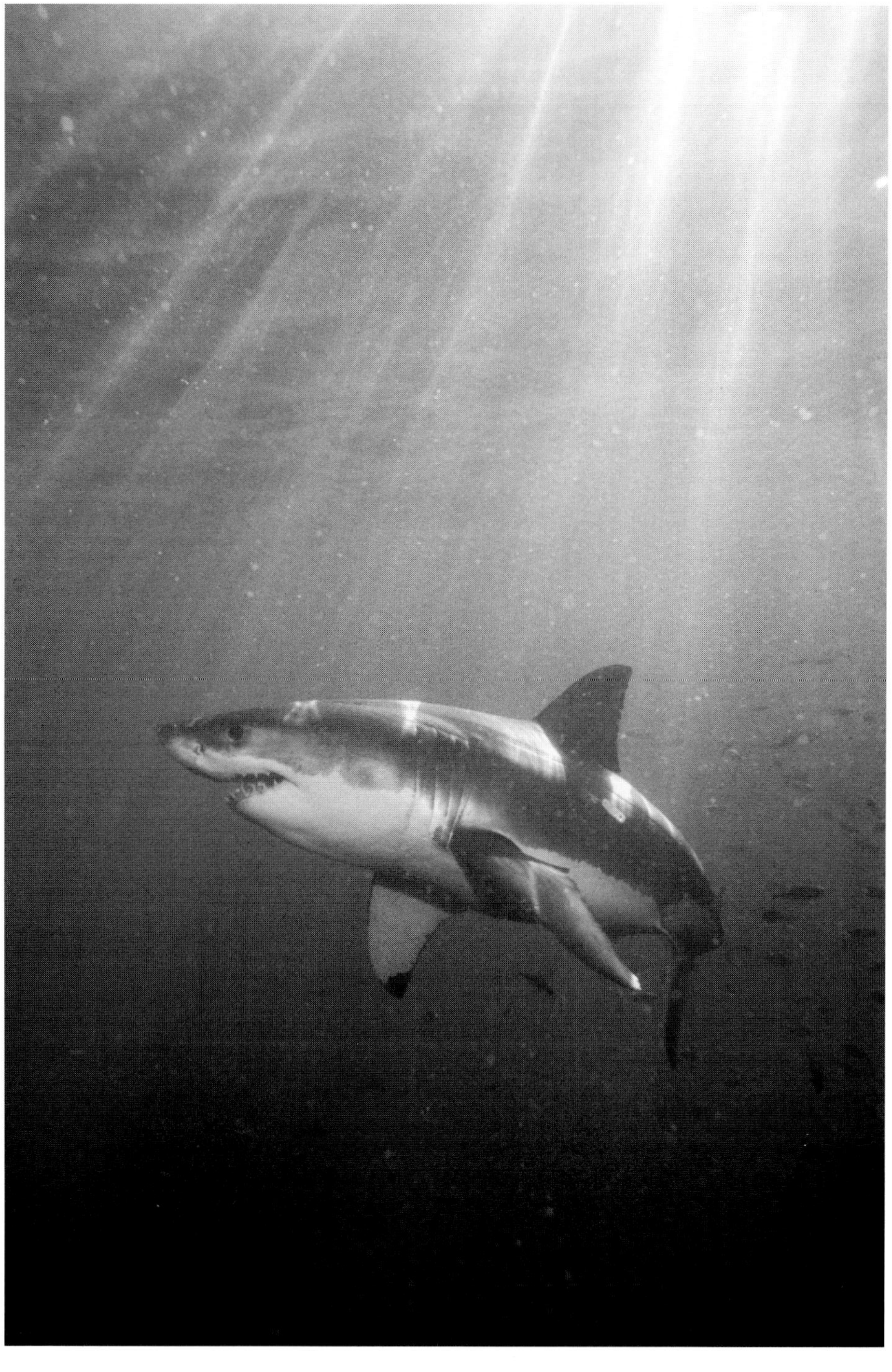

Great White shark, Neptune Islands, Australia

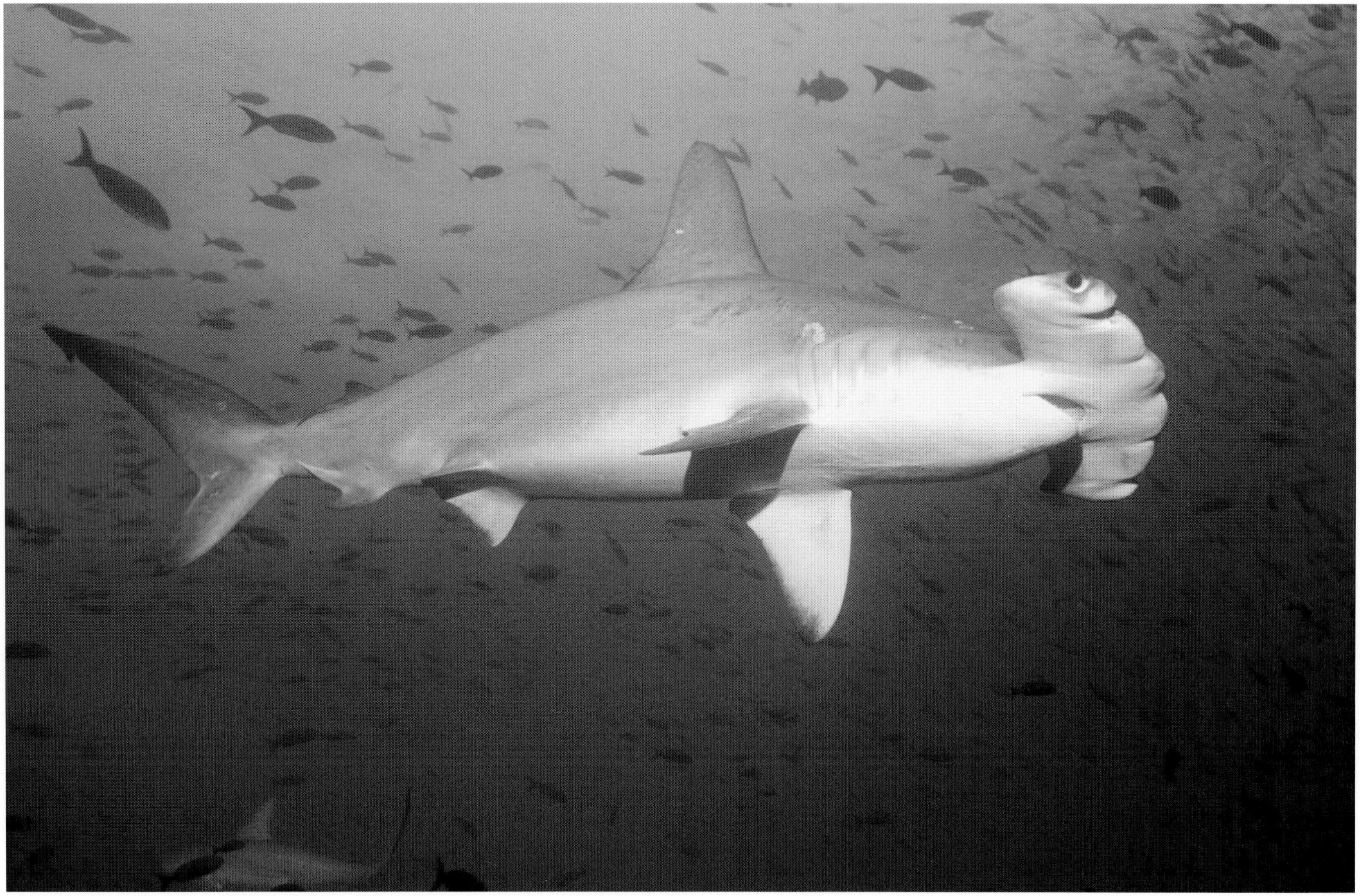

Scalloped Hammerhead shark, Darwin Island, Galapagos

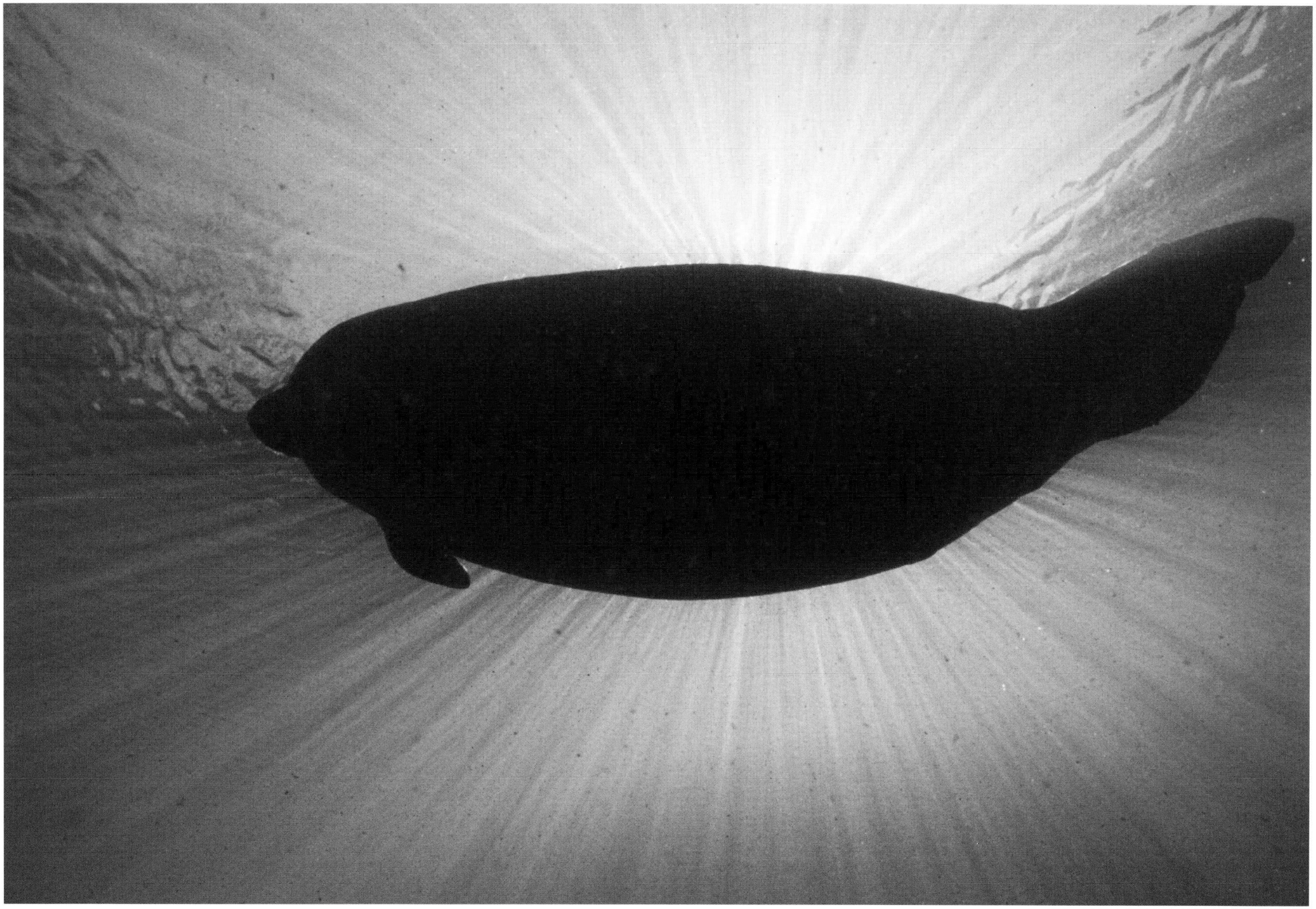

West Indian manatee, Homosassa, Florida

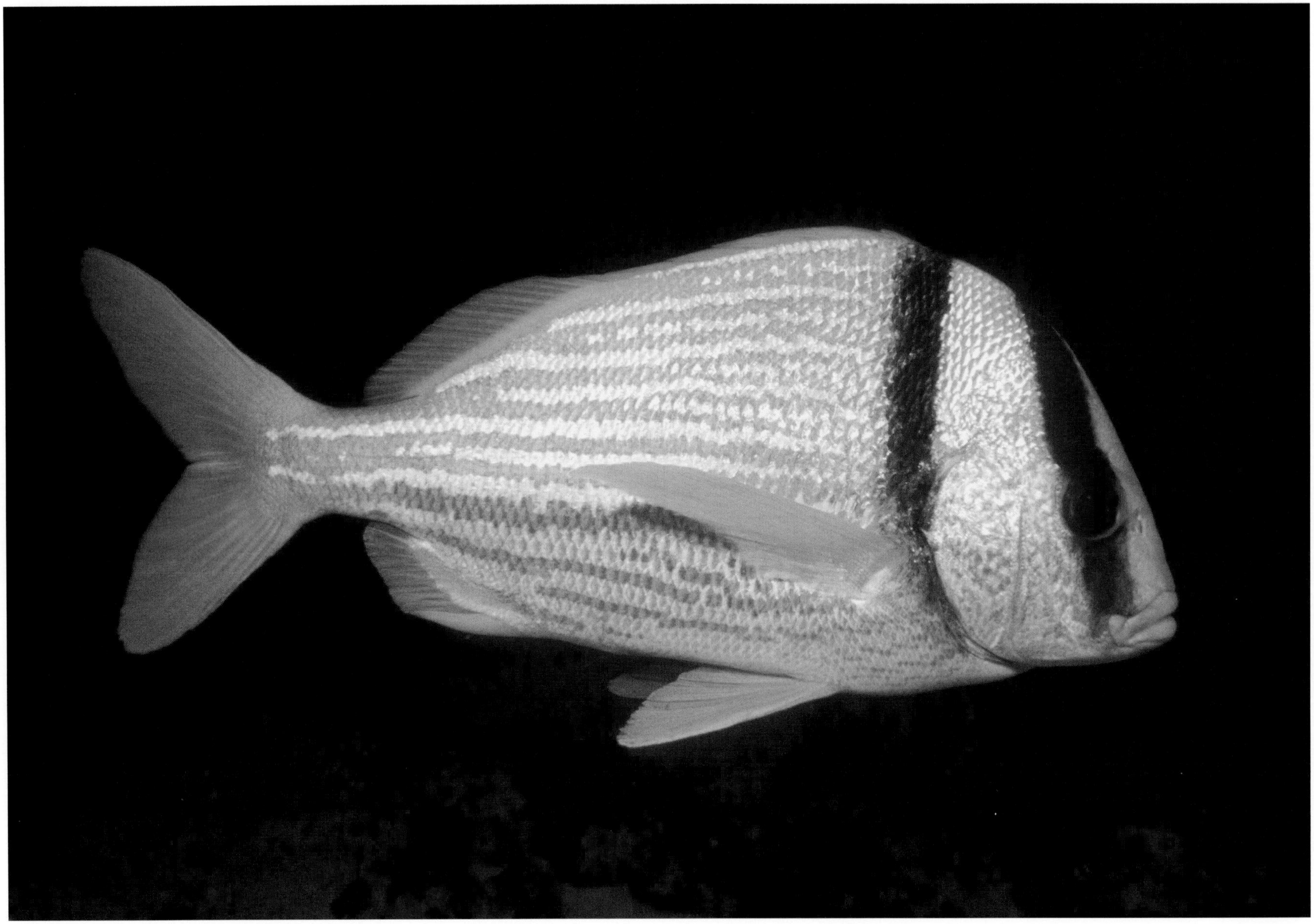

Porkfish, Cozumel, Mexico

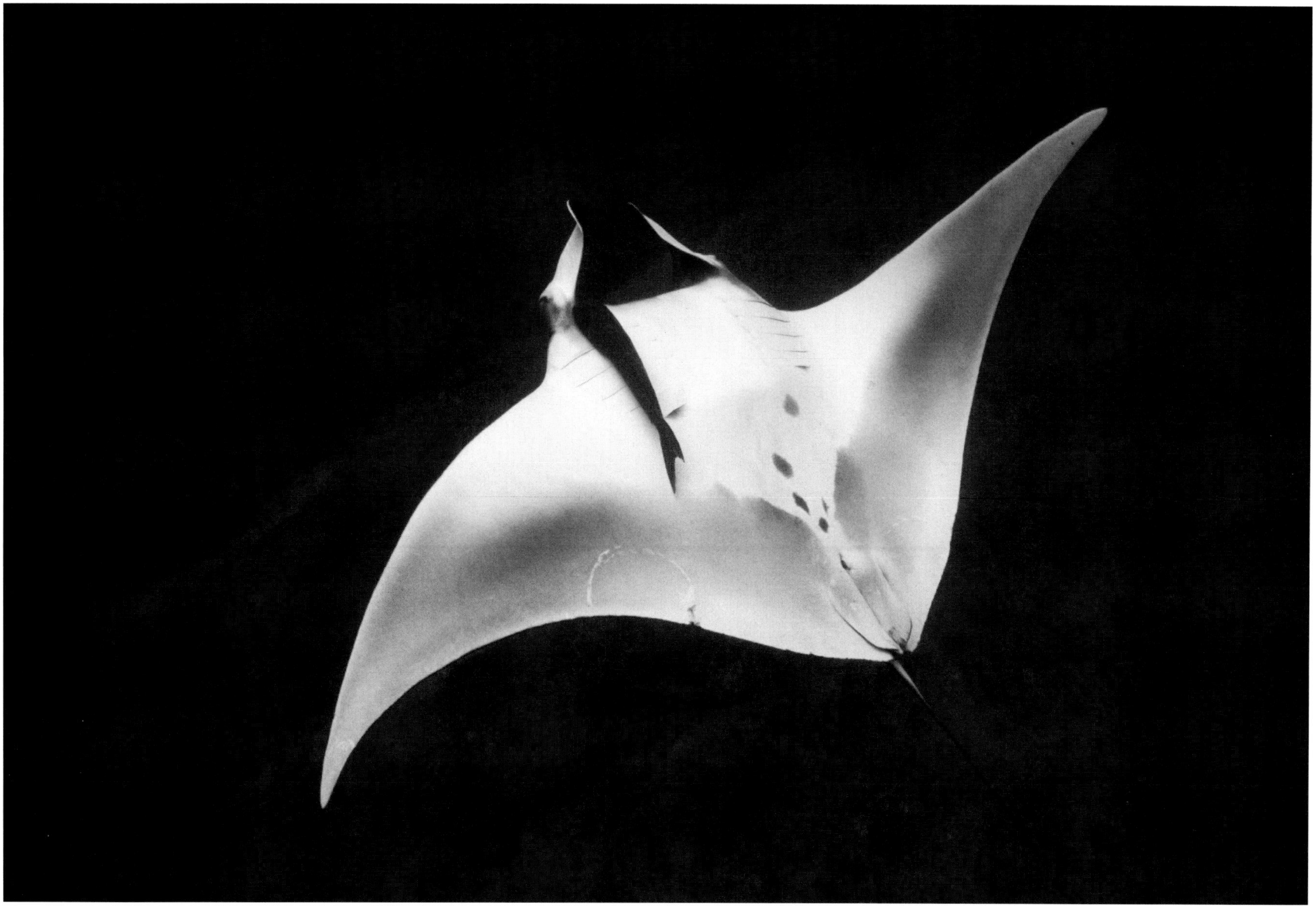

Atlantic Manta ray, Turks and Caicos Islands

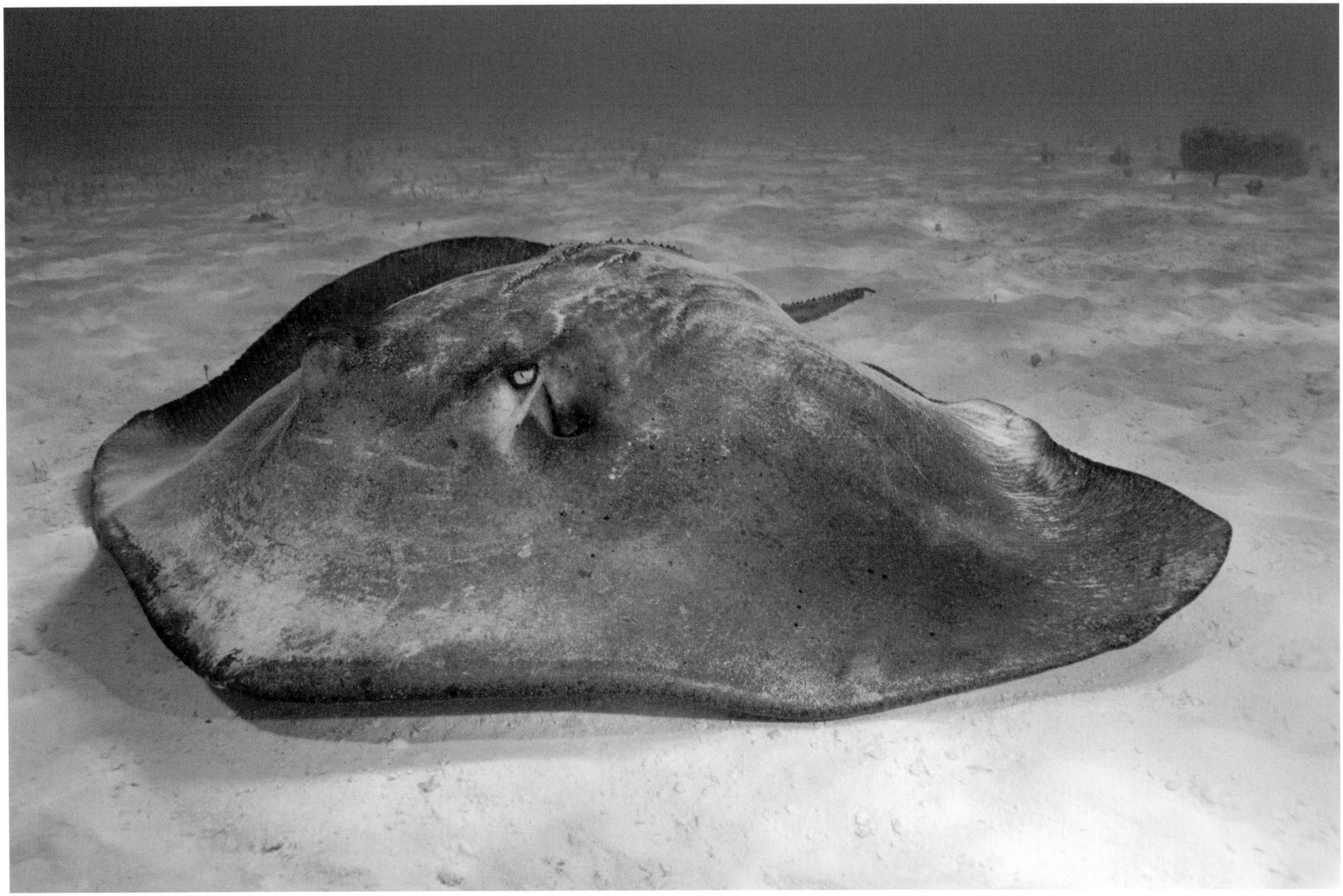

Southern stingray, Turks and Caicos Islands

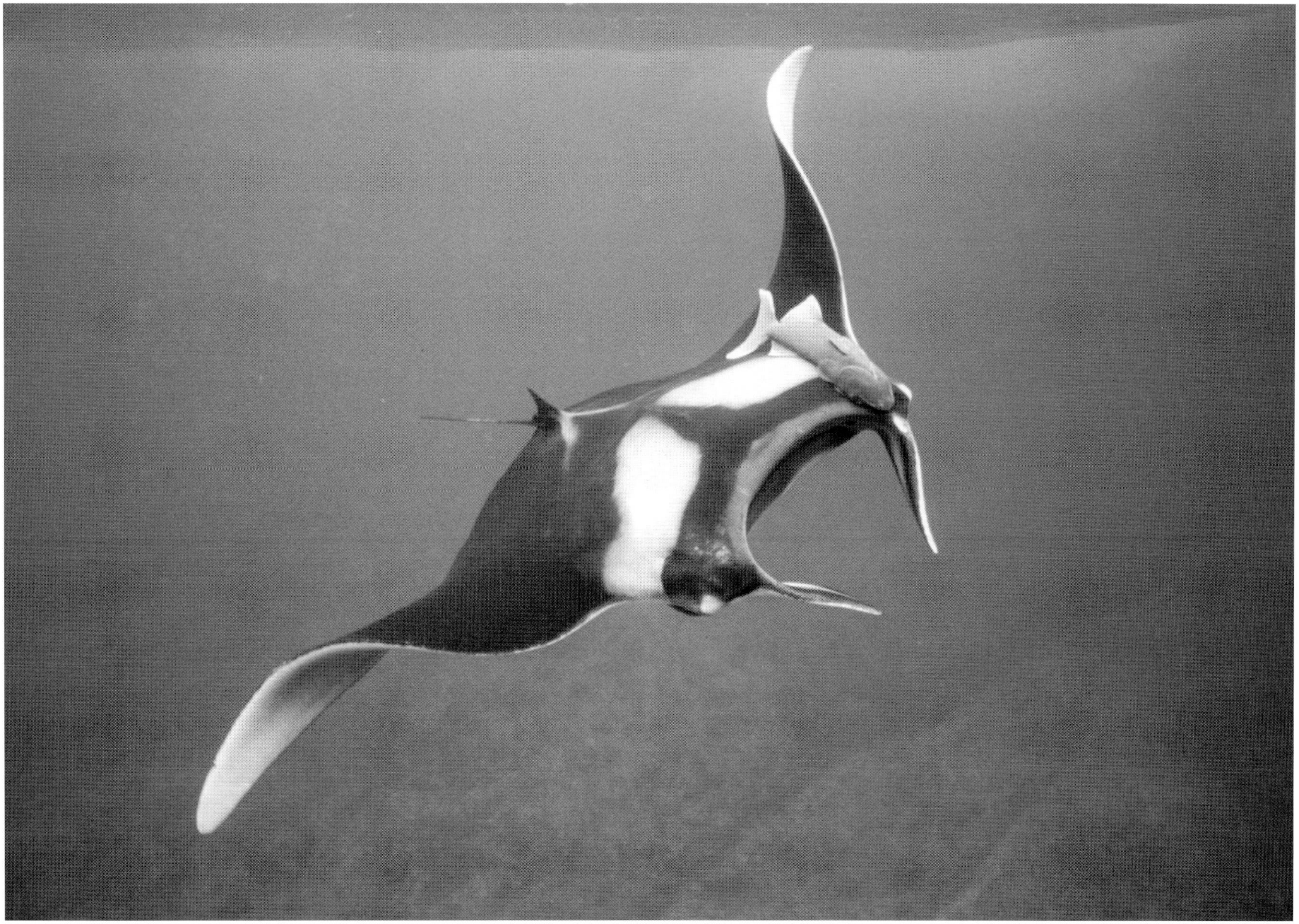

Atlantic Manta ray, Turks and Caicos Islands

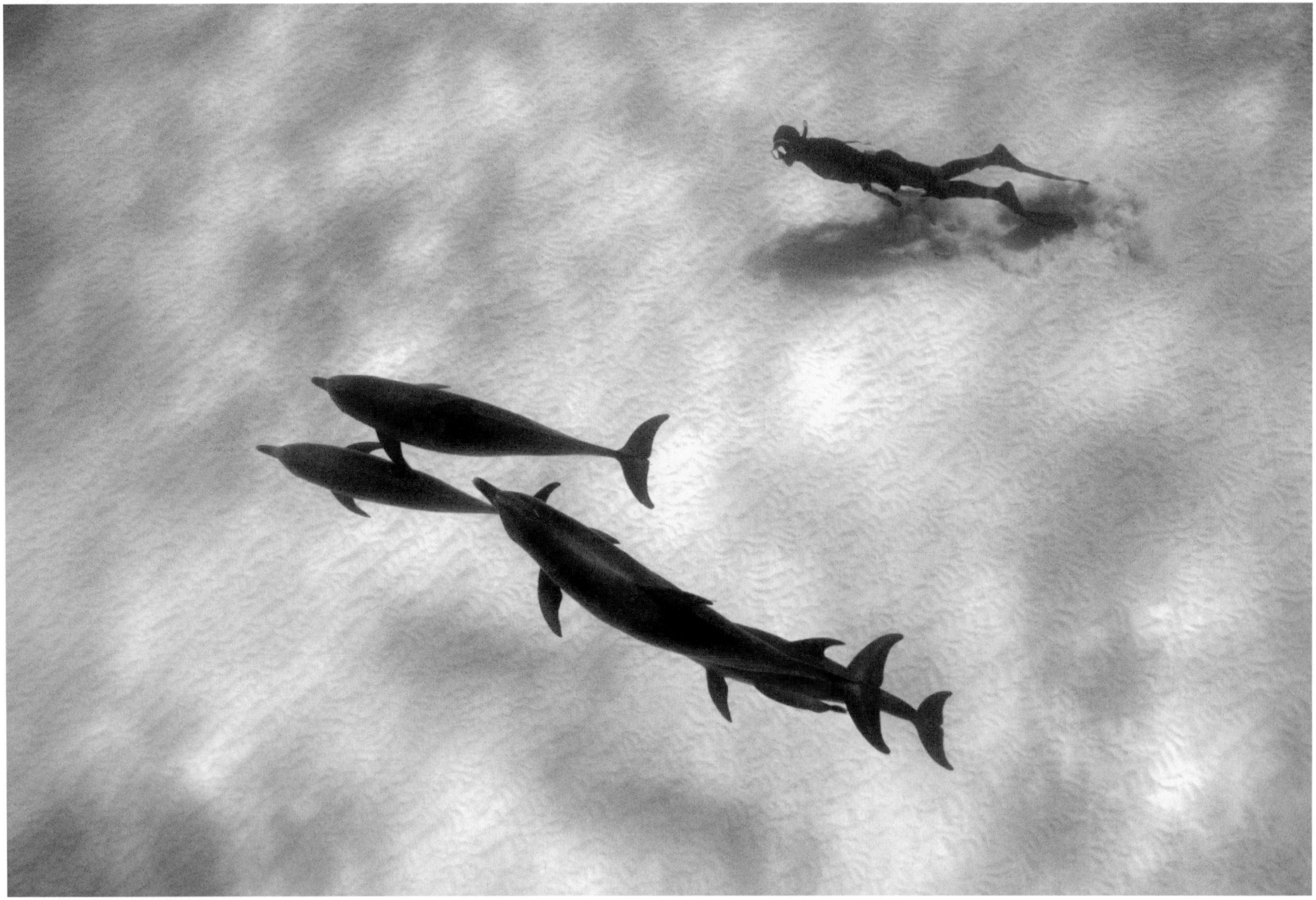

Freediver with Spotted dolphins, Bahamas

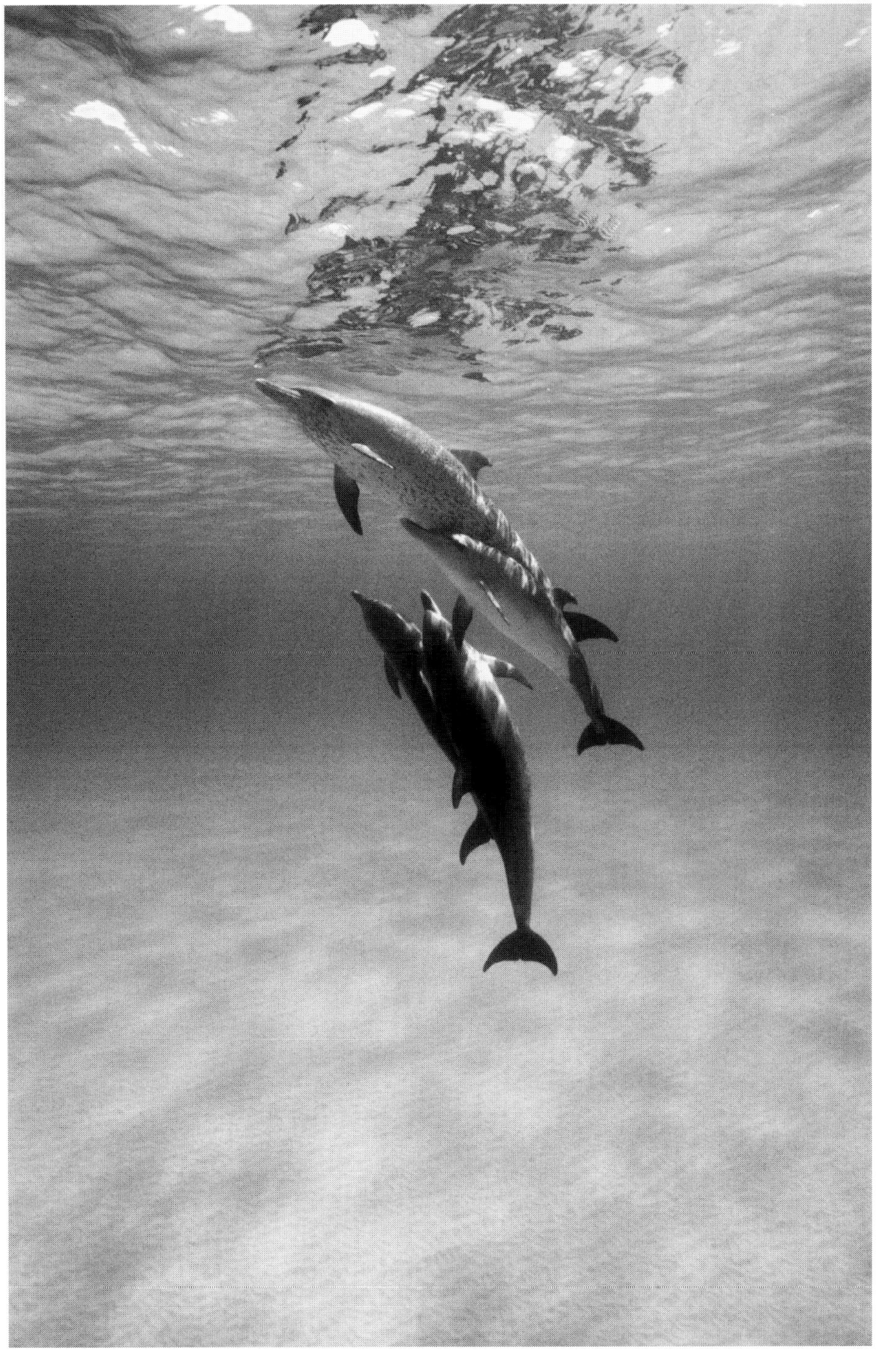

Atlantic Spotted dolphins playing,
Little Bahama Bank, Bahamas

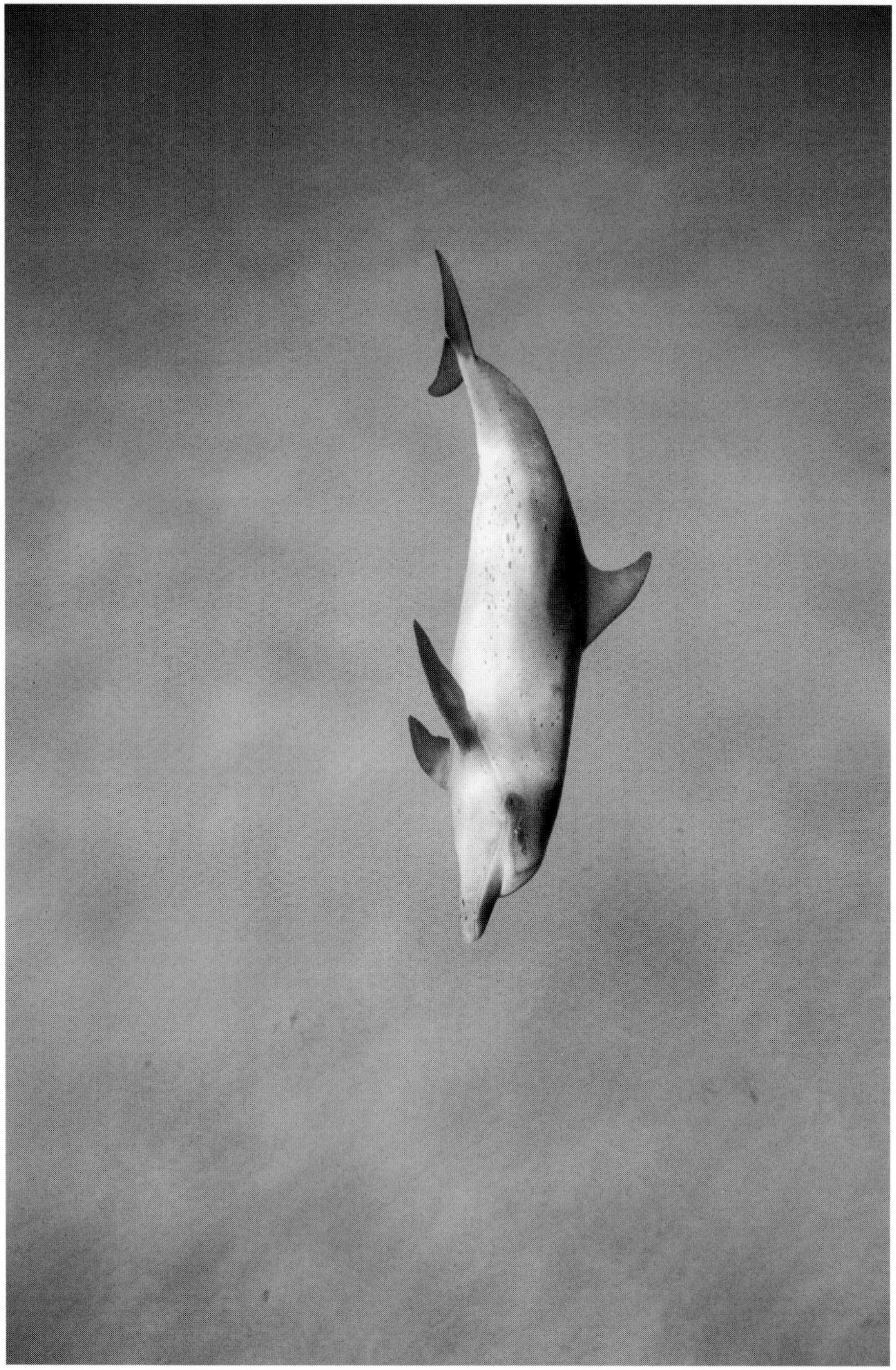

Juvenile Atlantic Spotted dolphin,
Little Bahama Bank, Bahamas

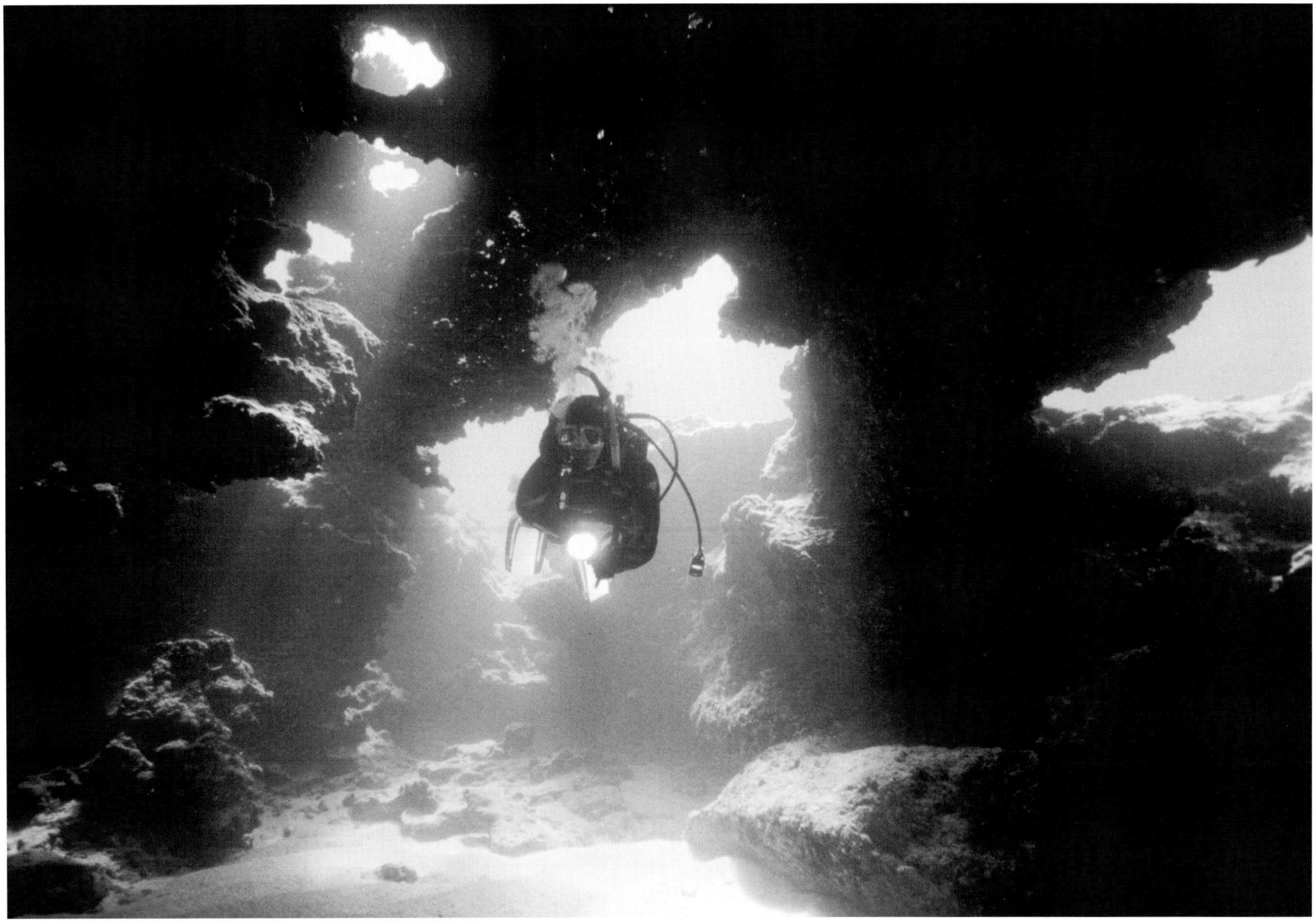

Diver in coral cavern, Midway Atoll

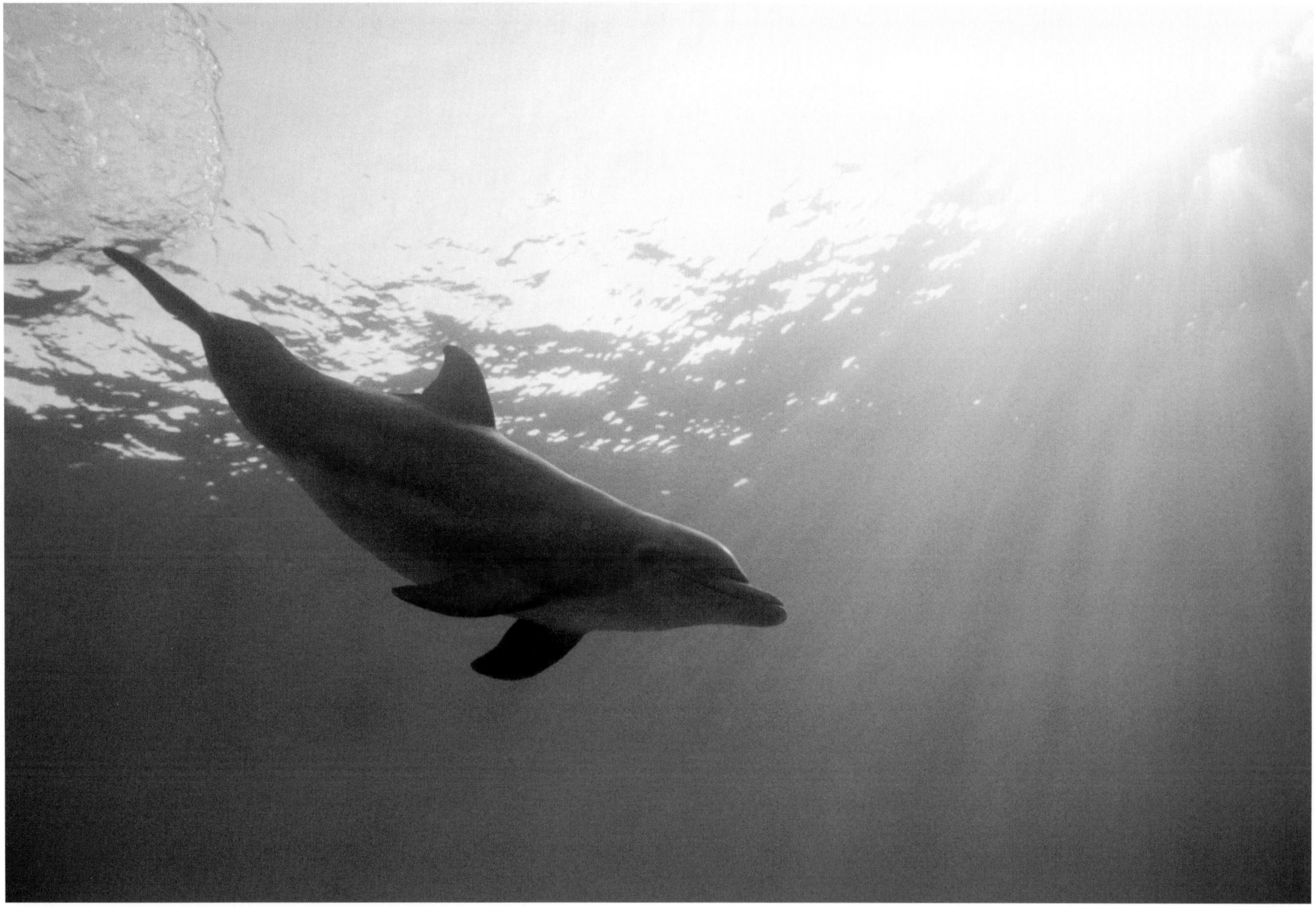

Bottlenosed dolphin, Roatan, Honduras

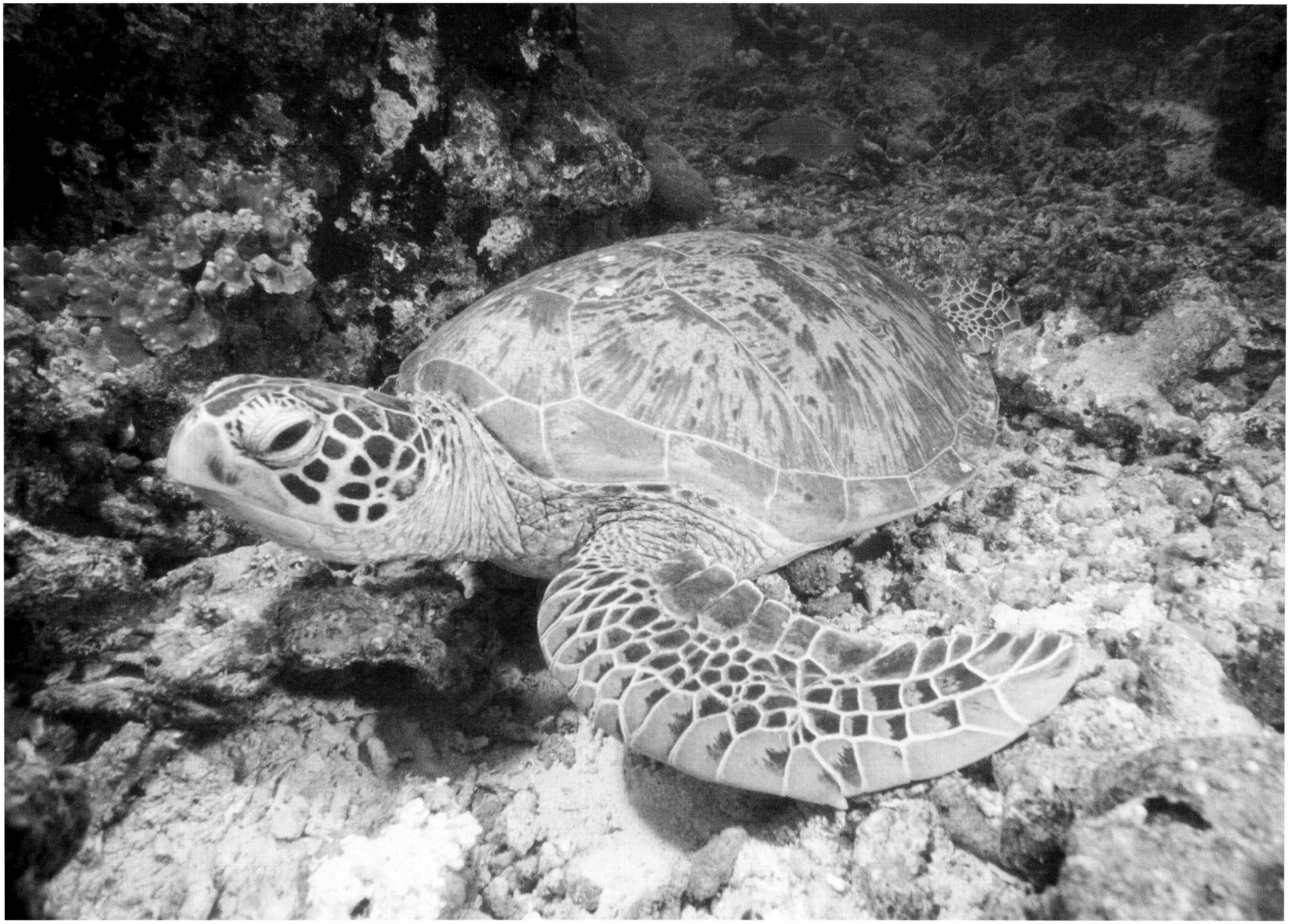

Green sea tutle, Sipadan Island, Malaysia

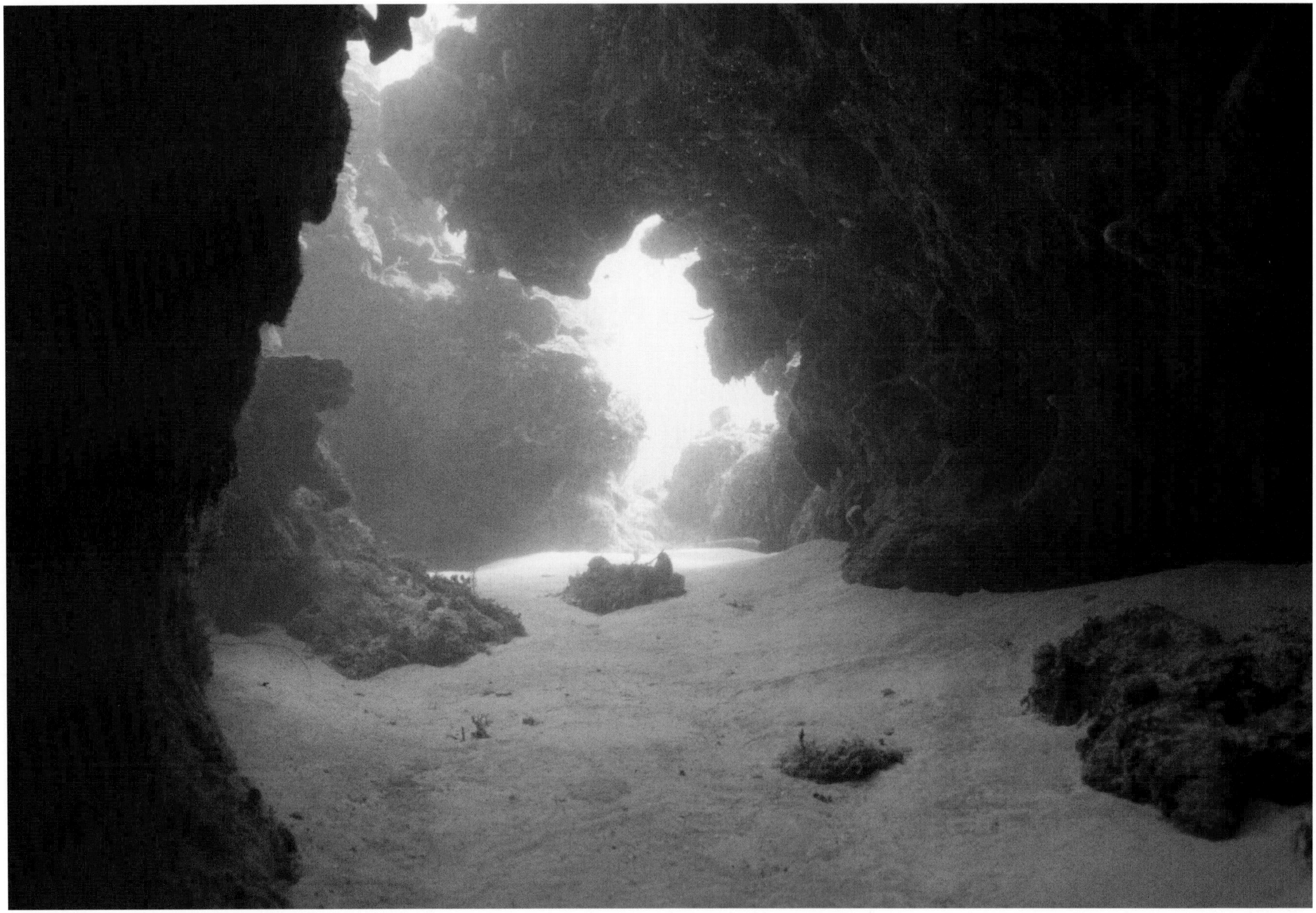

Coral cavern, Turks and Caicos Islands

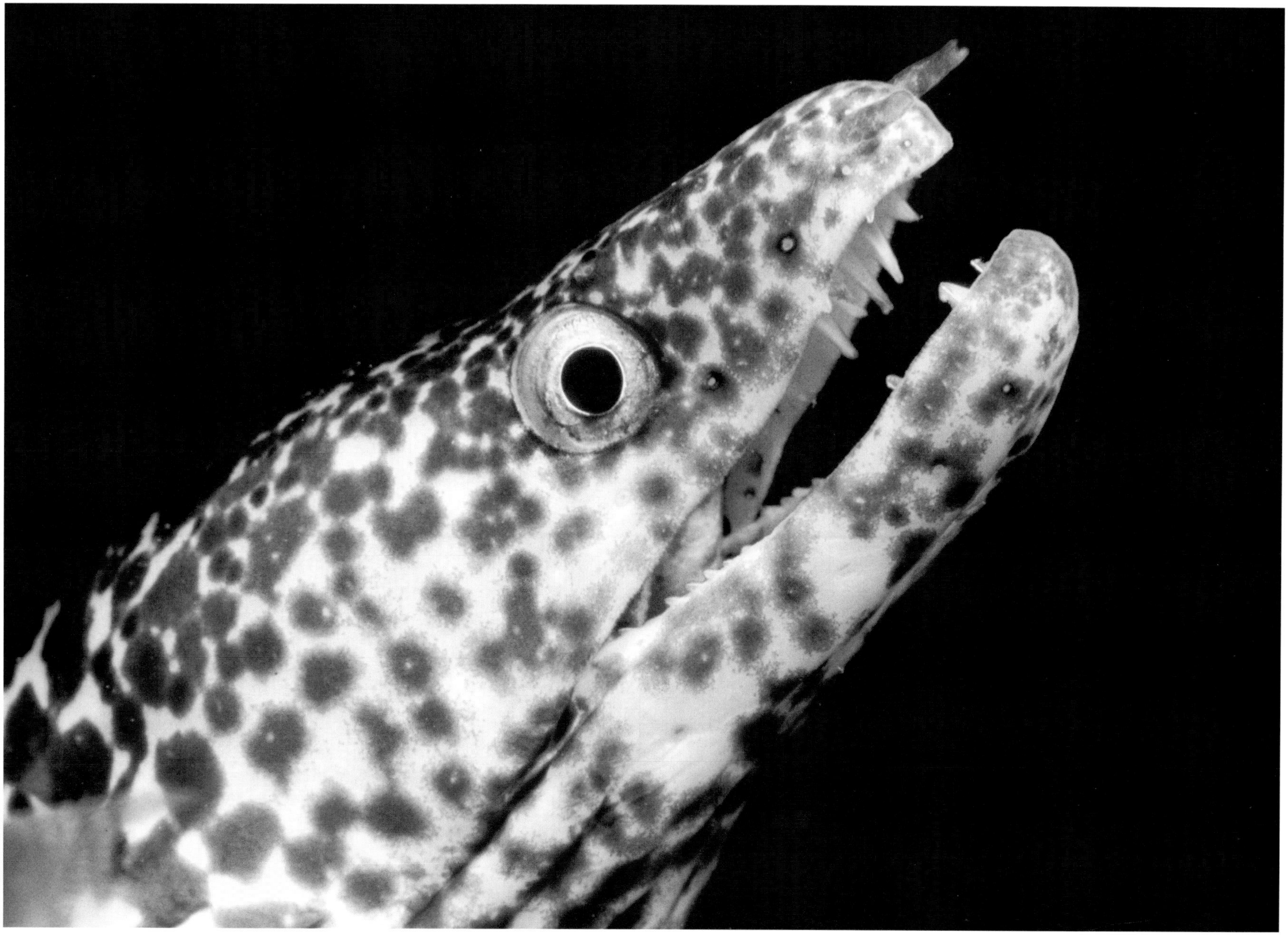

Spotted Moray eel, St. Croix, U.S. Virgin Islands

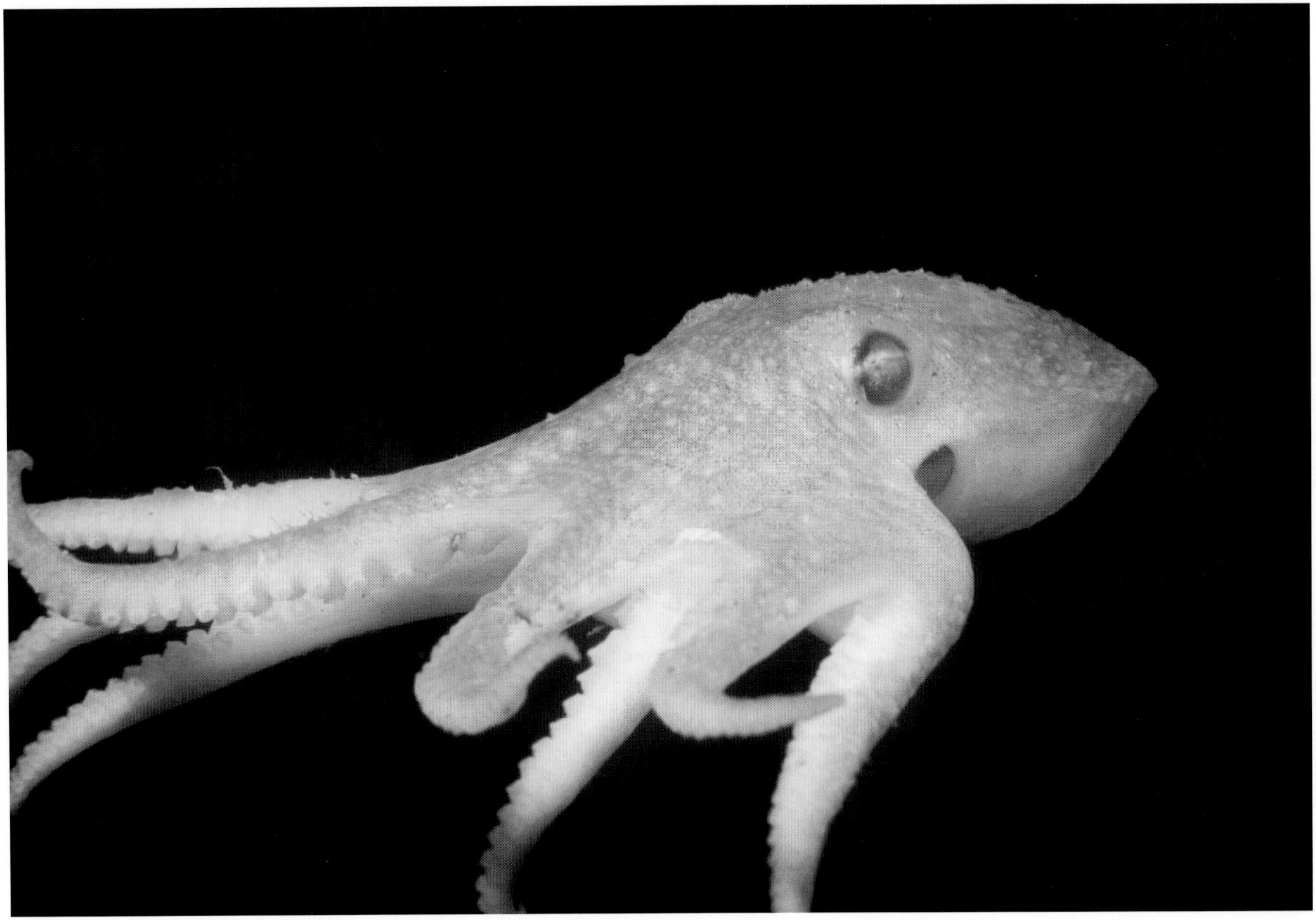

Arctic octopus, Massachusetts Bay

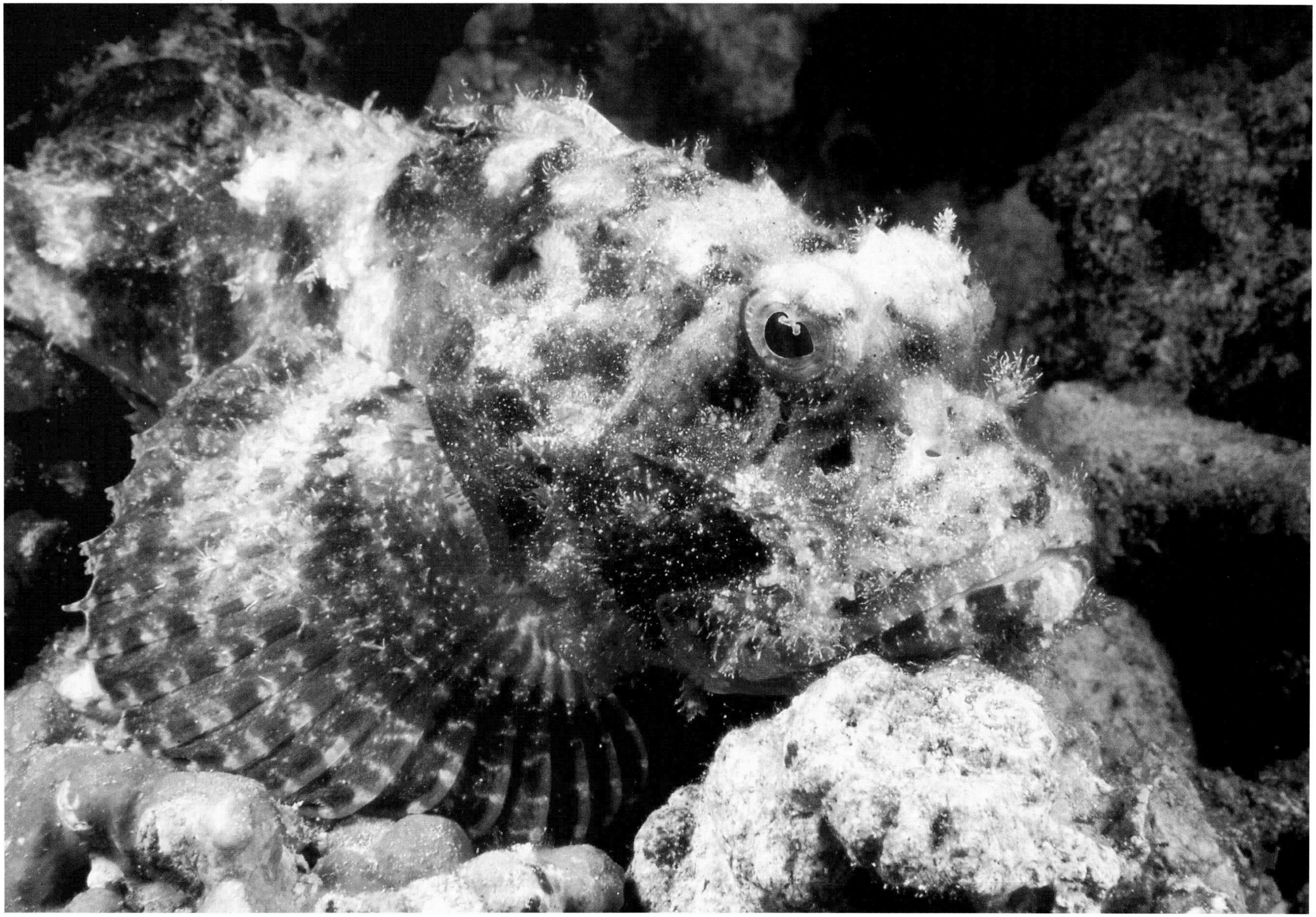

Scorpionfish, Midway Atoll

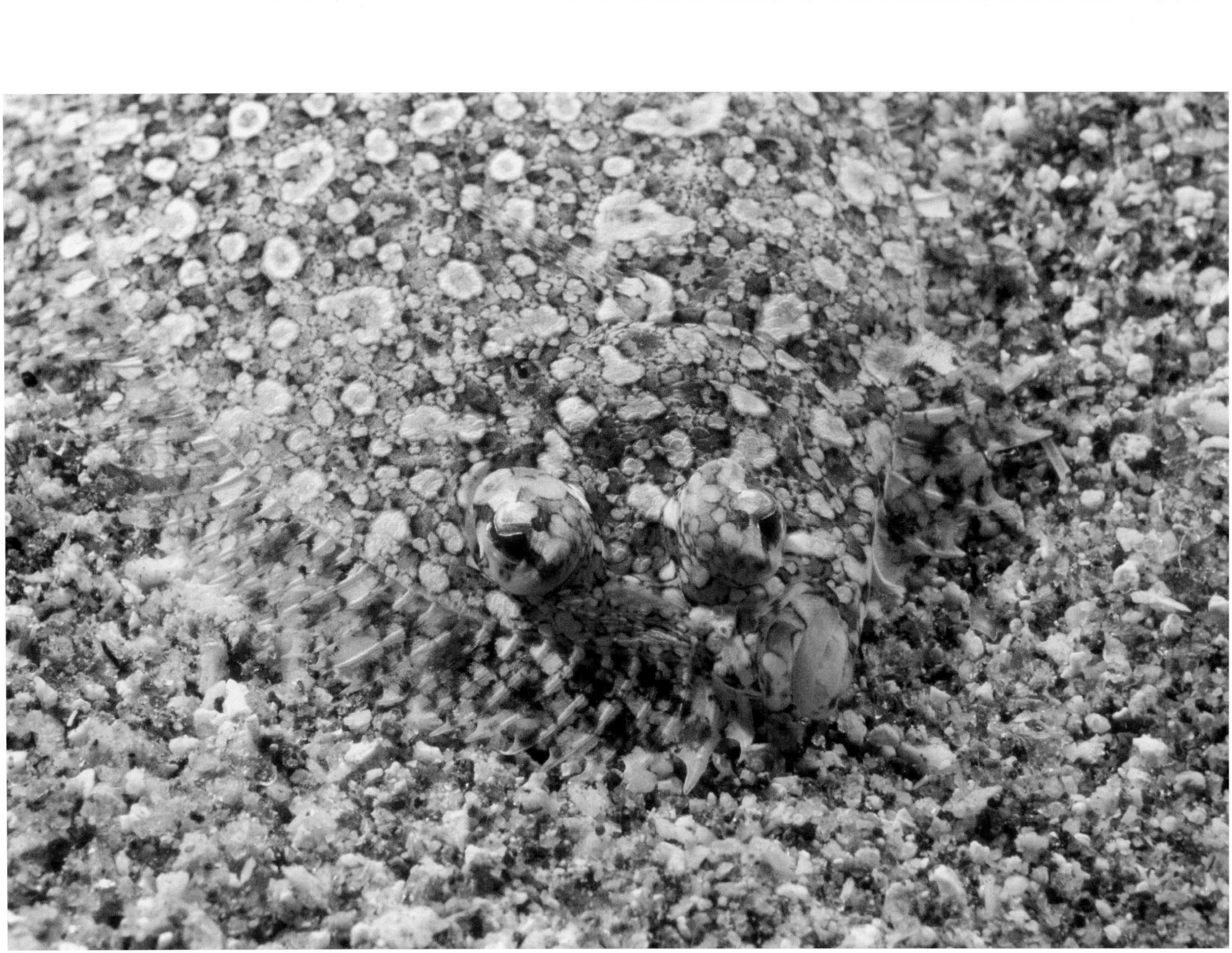

Flounder on sand, St. Lucia

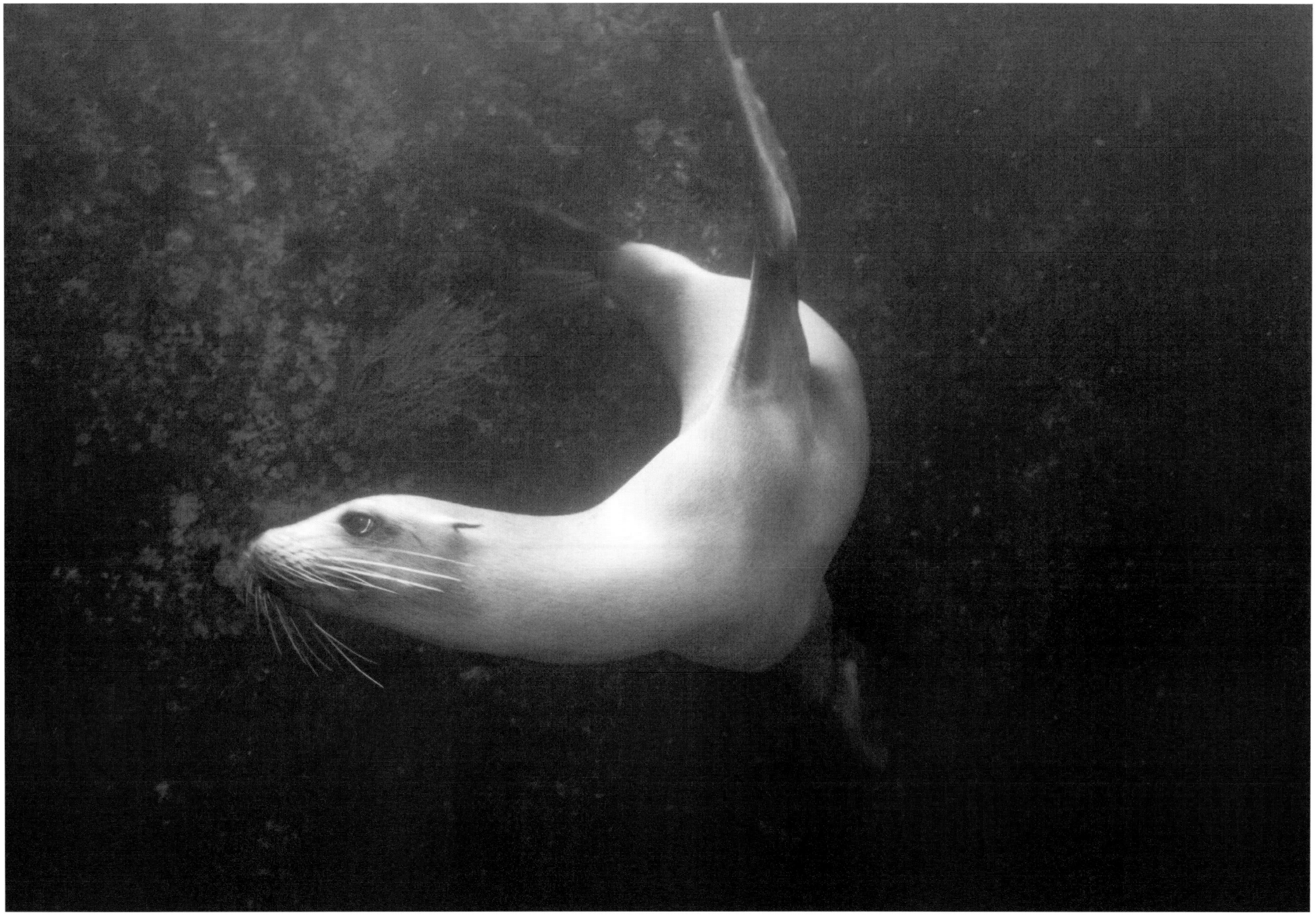

Sea lion, Cousin's Rock, Galapagos

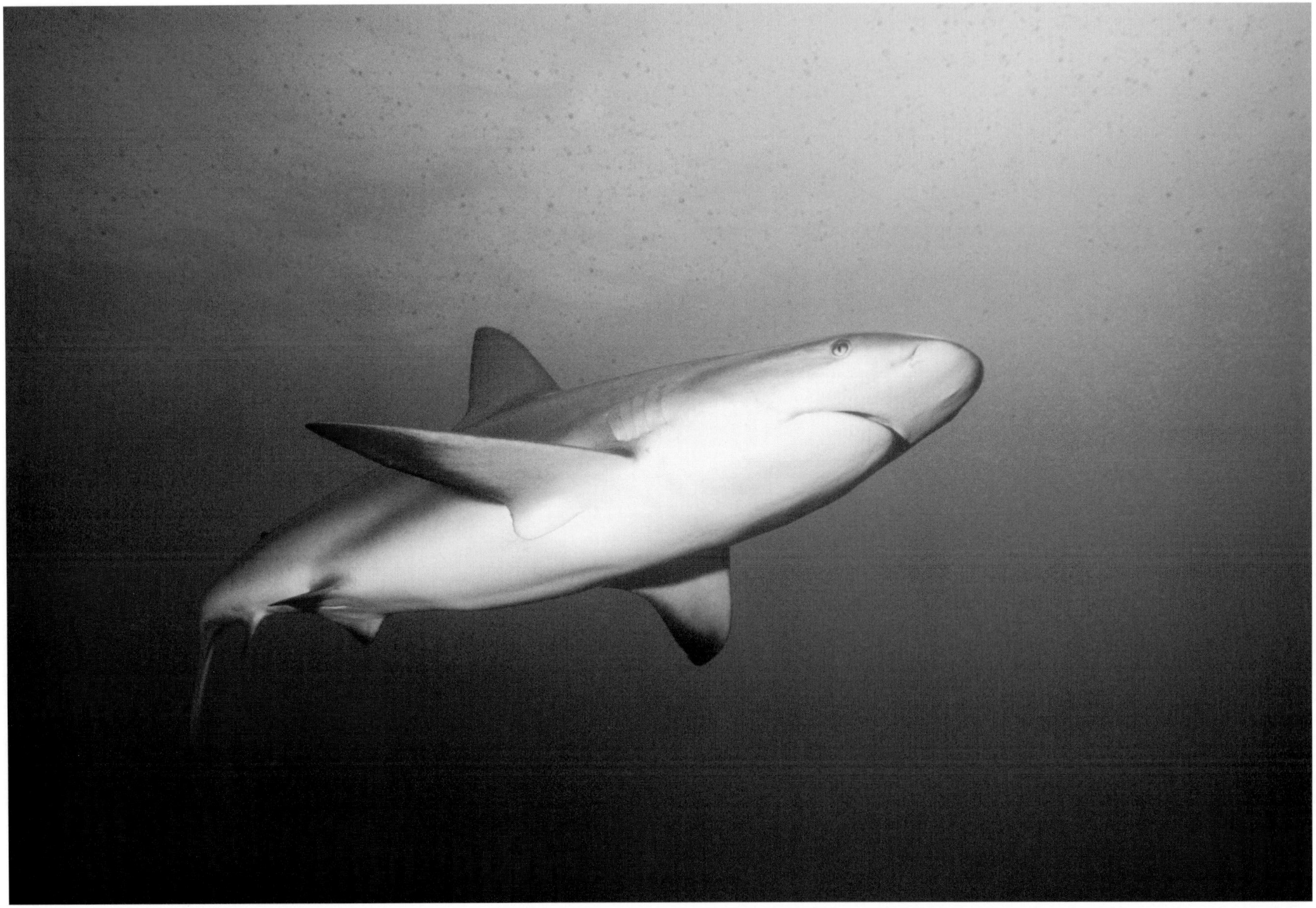

Caribbean Reef shark, Bahamas

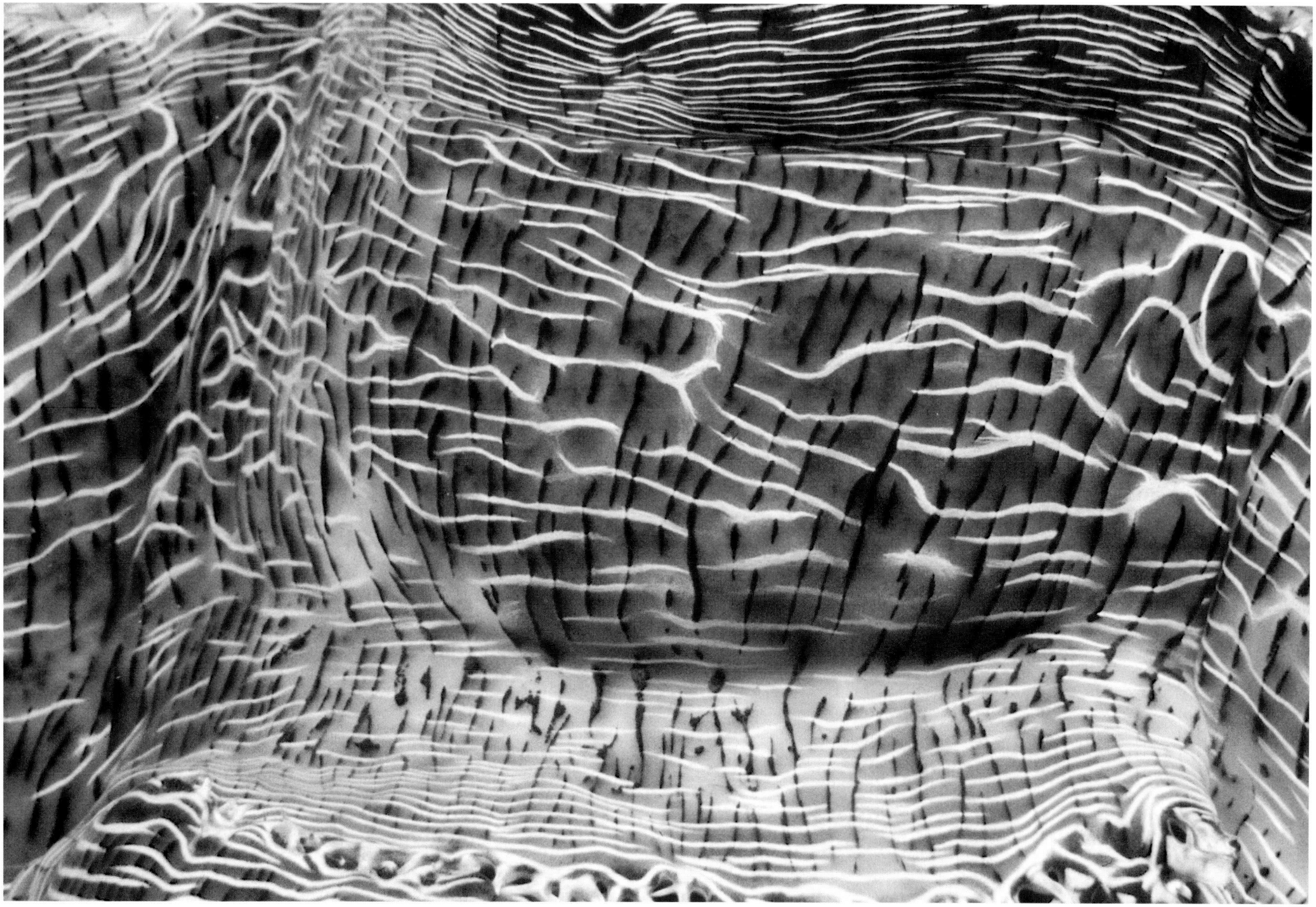

Tridacna clam mantle, Kosrae, Micronesia

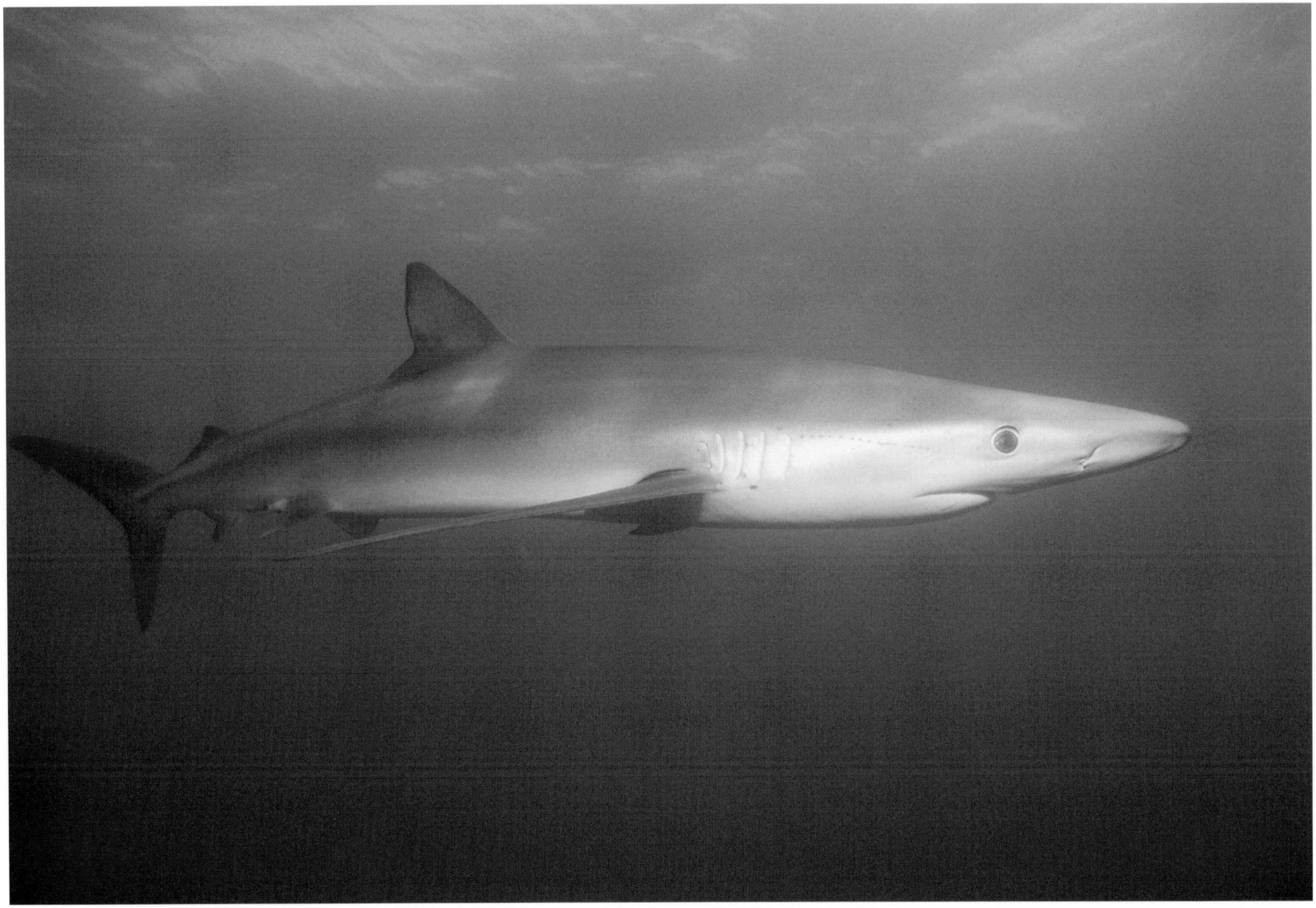

Blue shark, Rhode Island

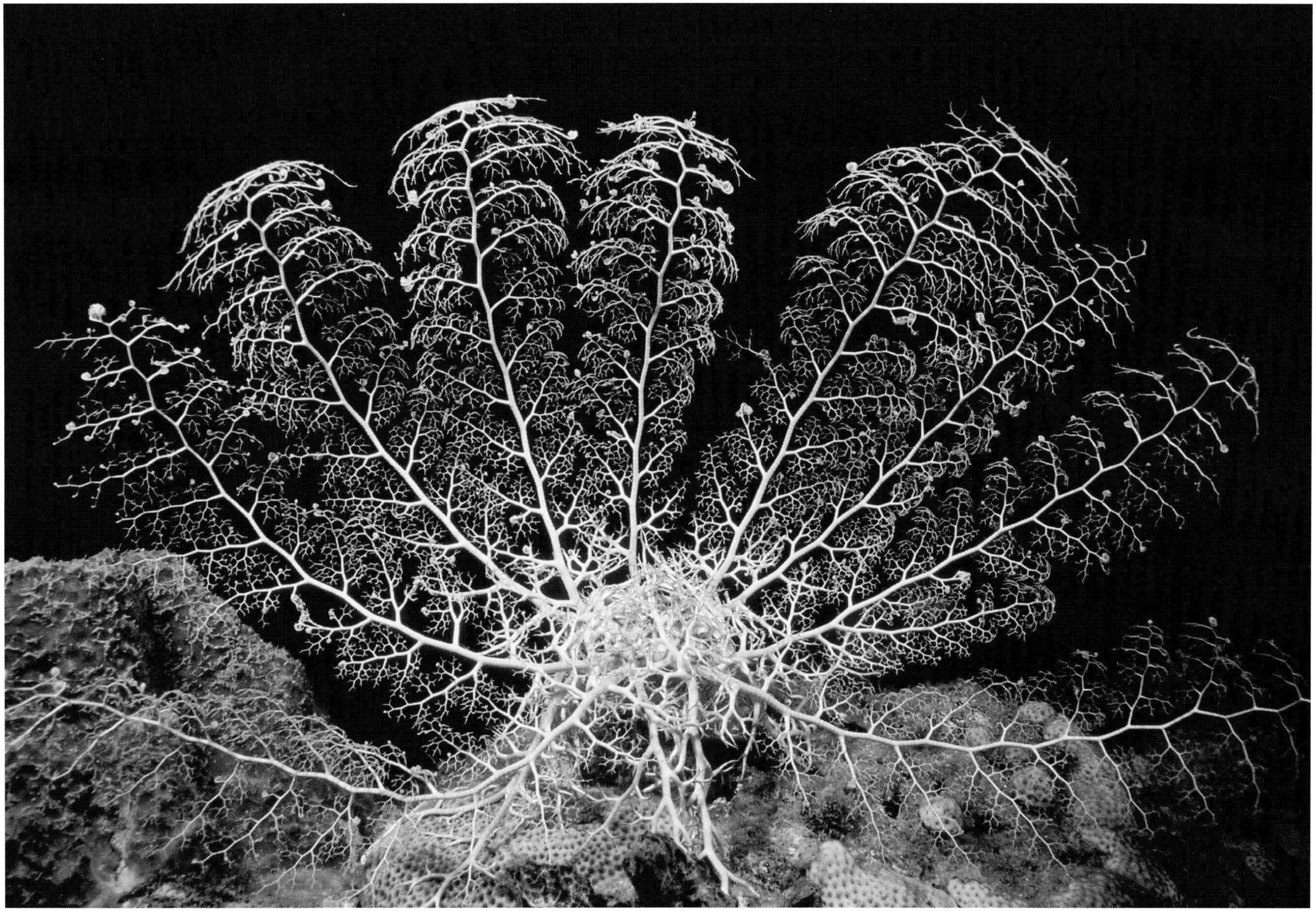

Basket star, Dominica

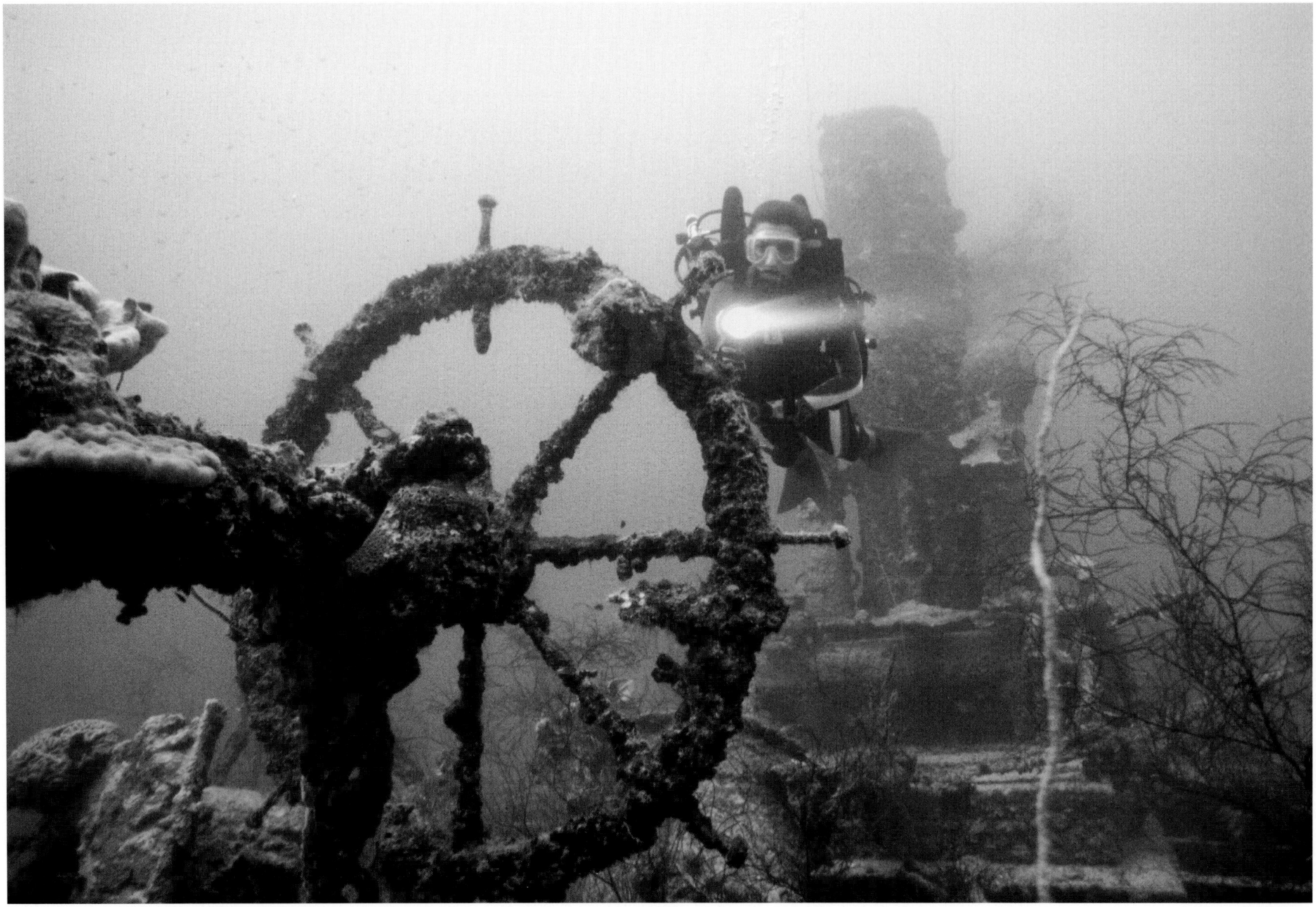

Bigej Wreck, Kwajalein Atoll, Marshall Islands

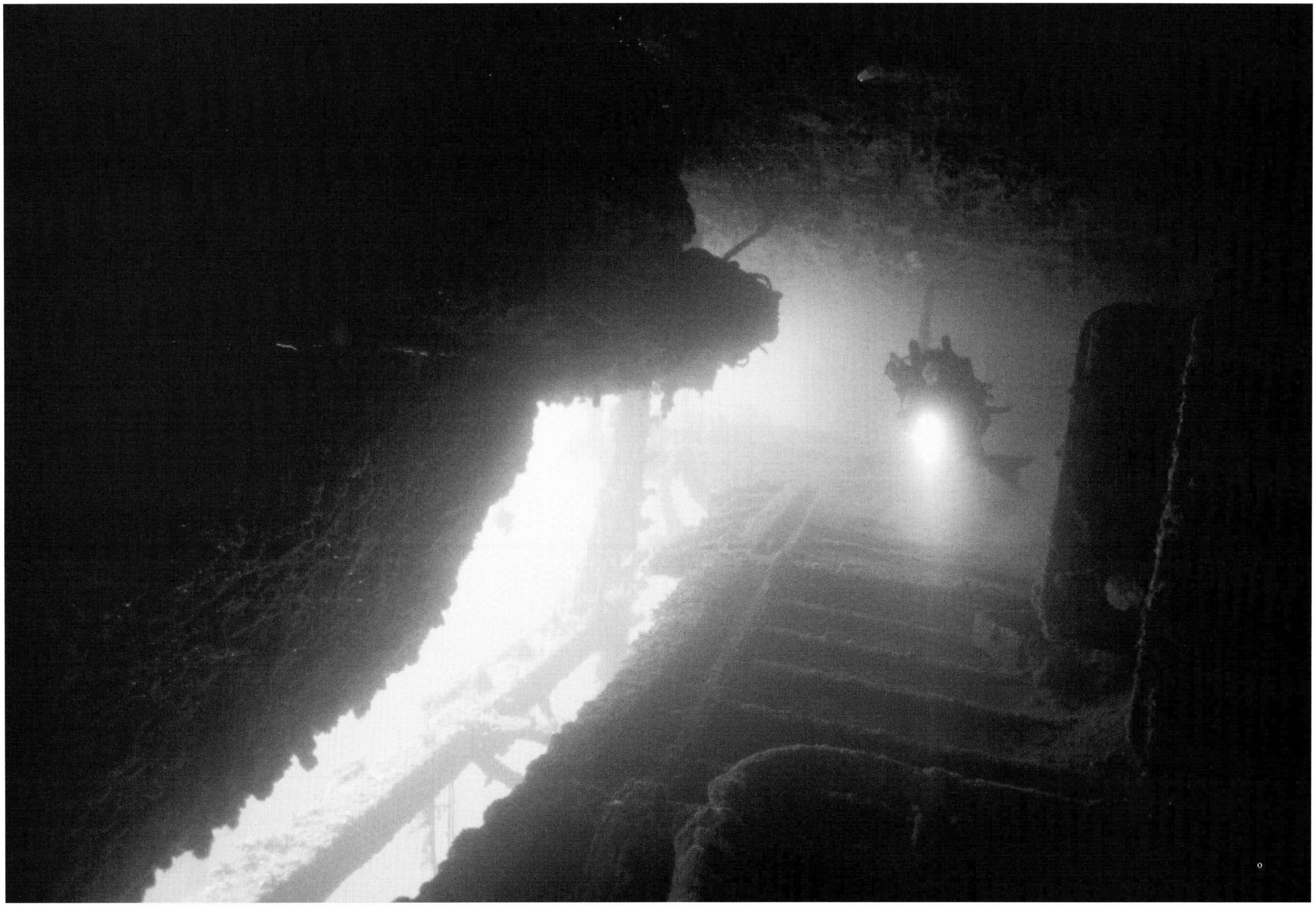

Prinz Eugen wreck, Kwajalein Atoll, Marshall Islands

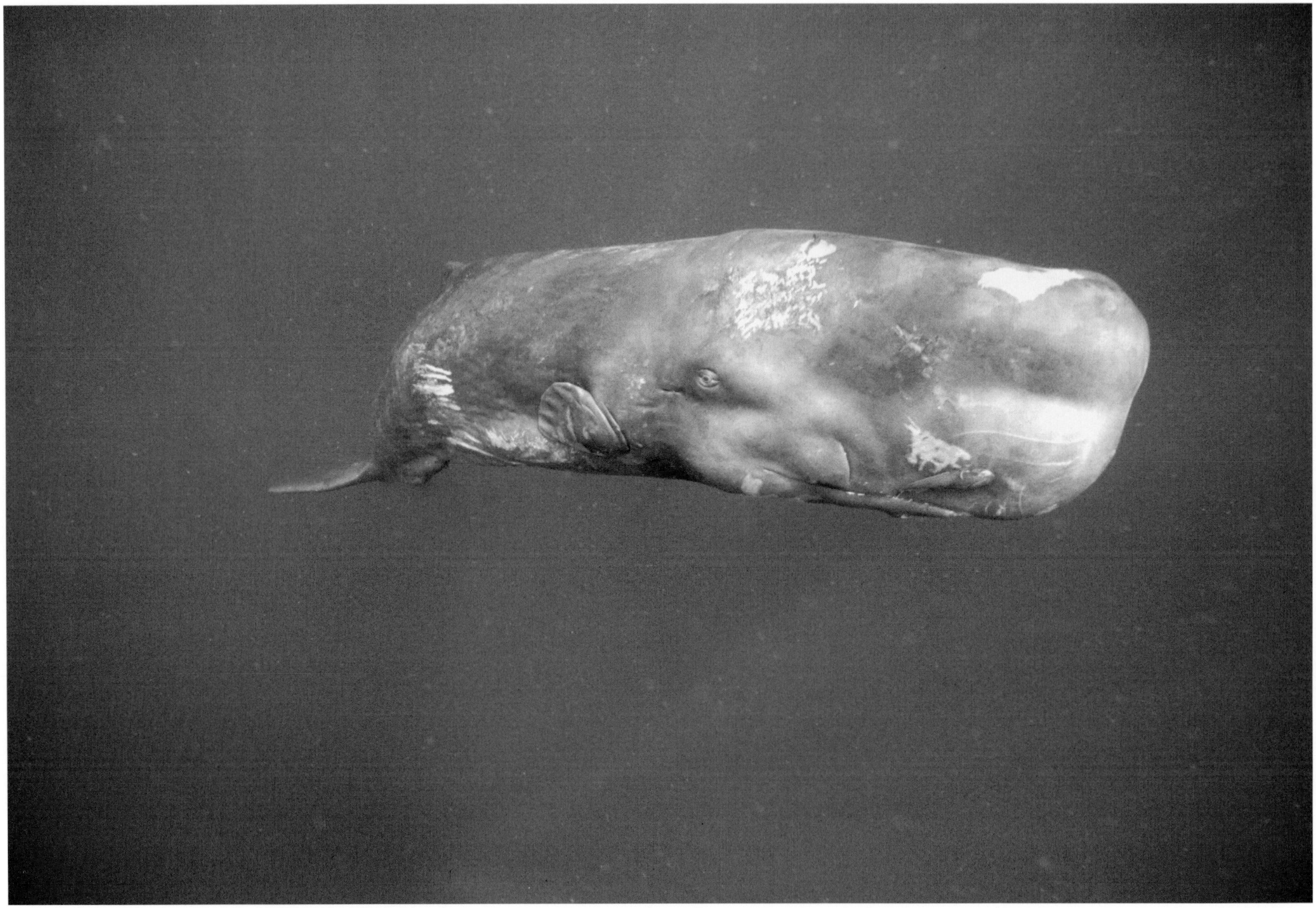

Sperm whale, Dominica

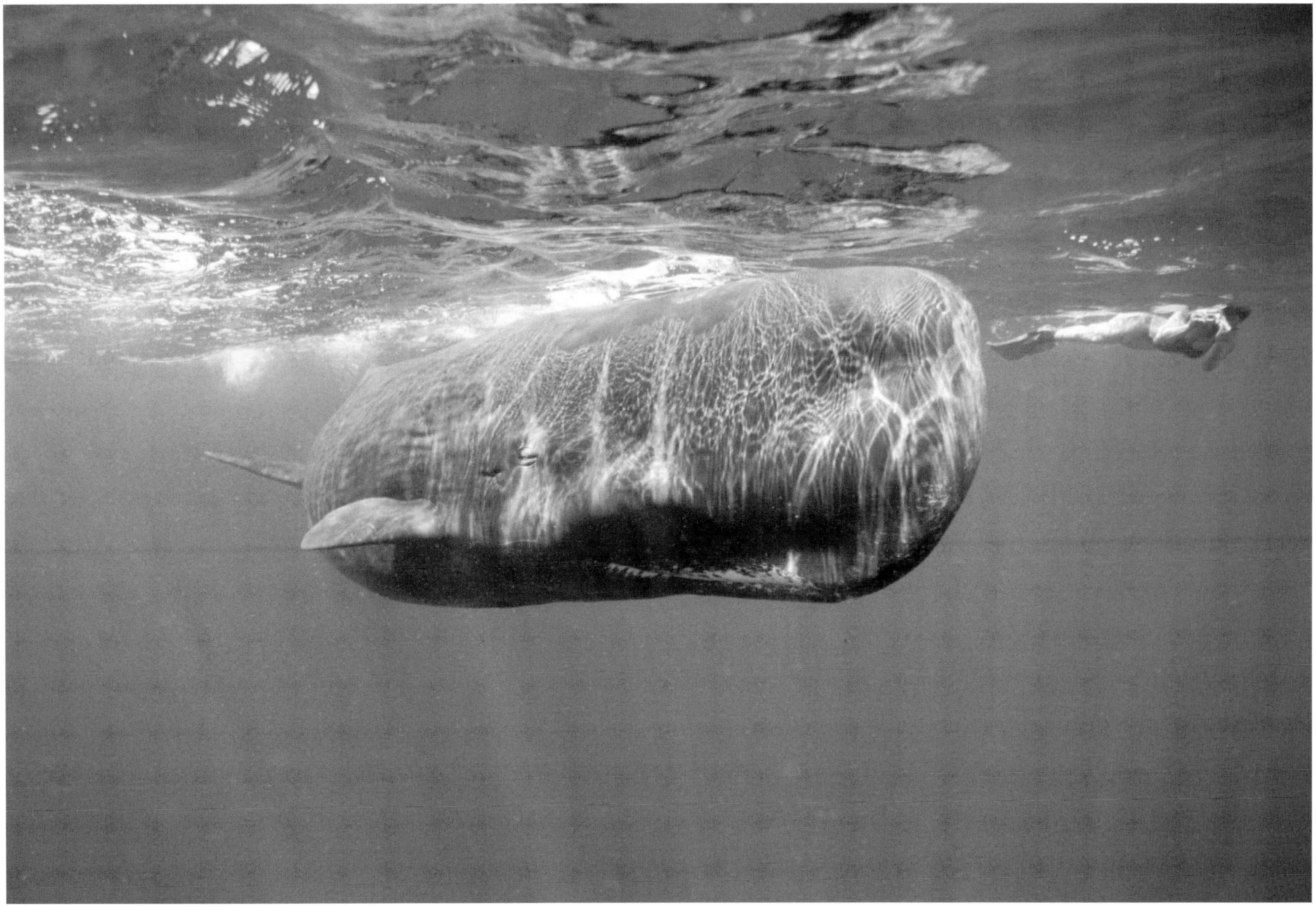

Sperm whale, Dominica

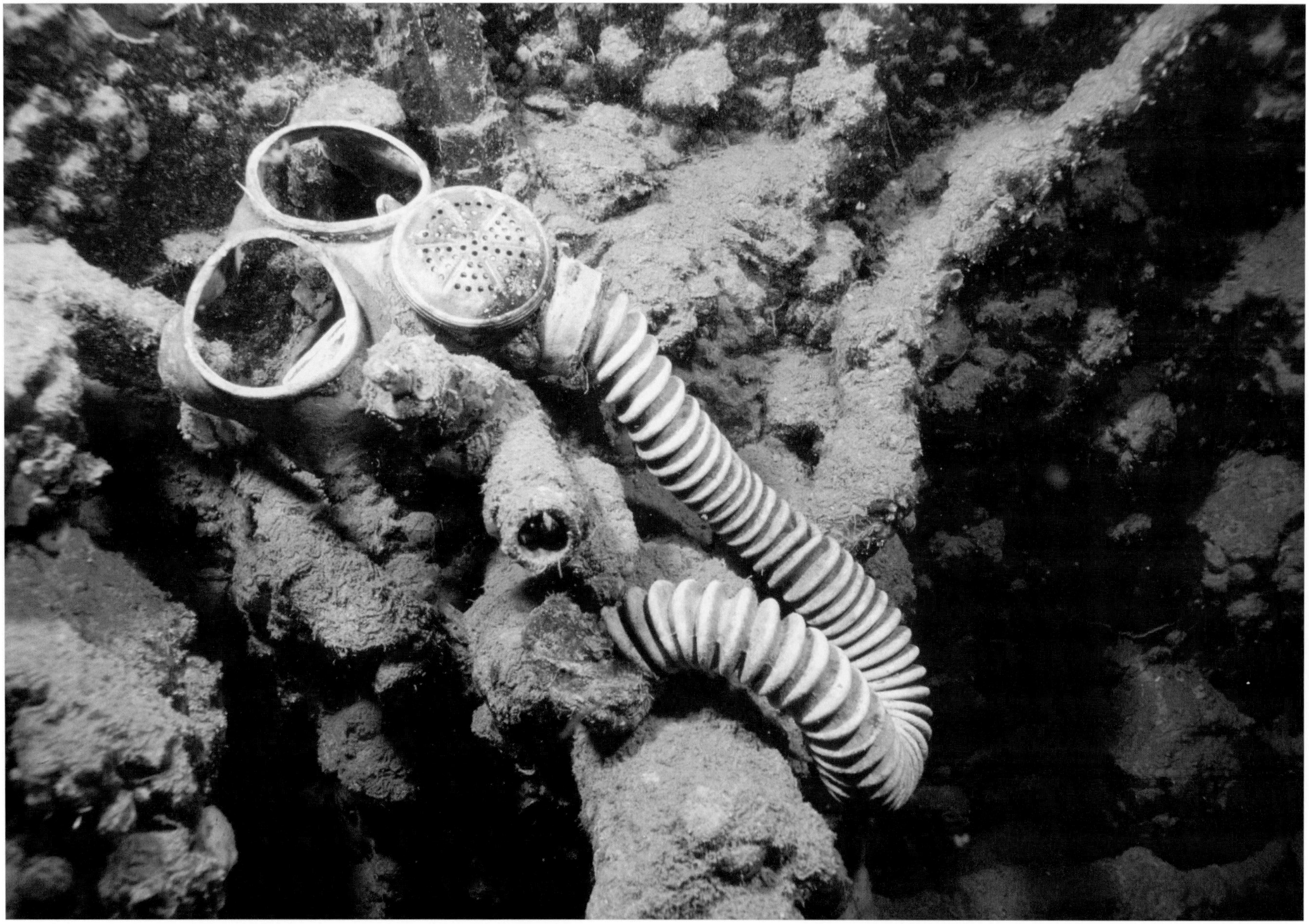

Gas mask, Kiyozumi Maru, Chuuck Lagoon, Micronesia

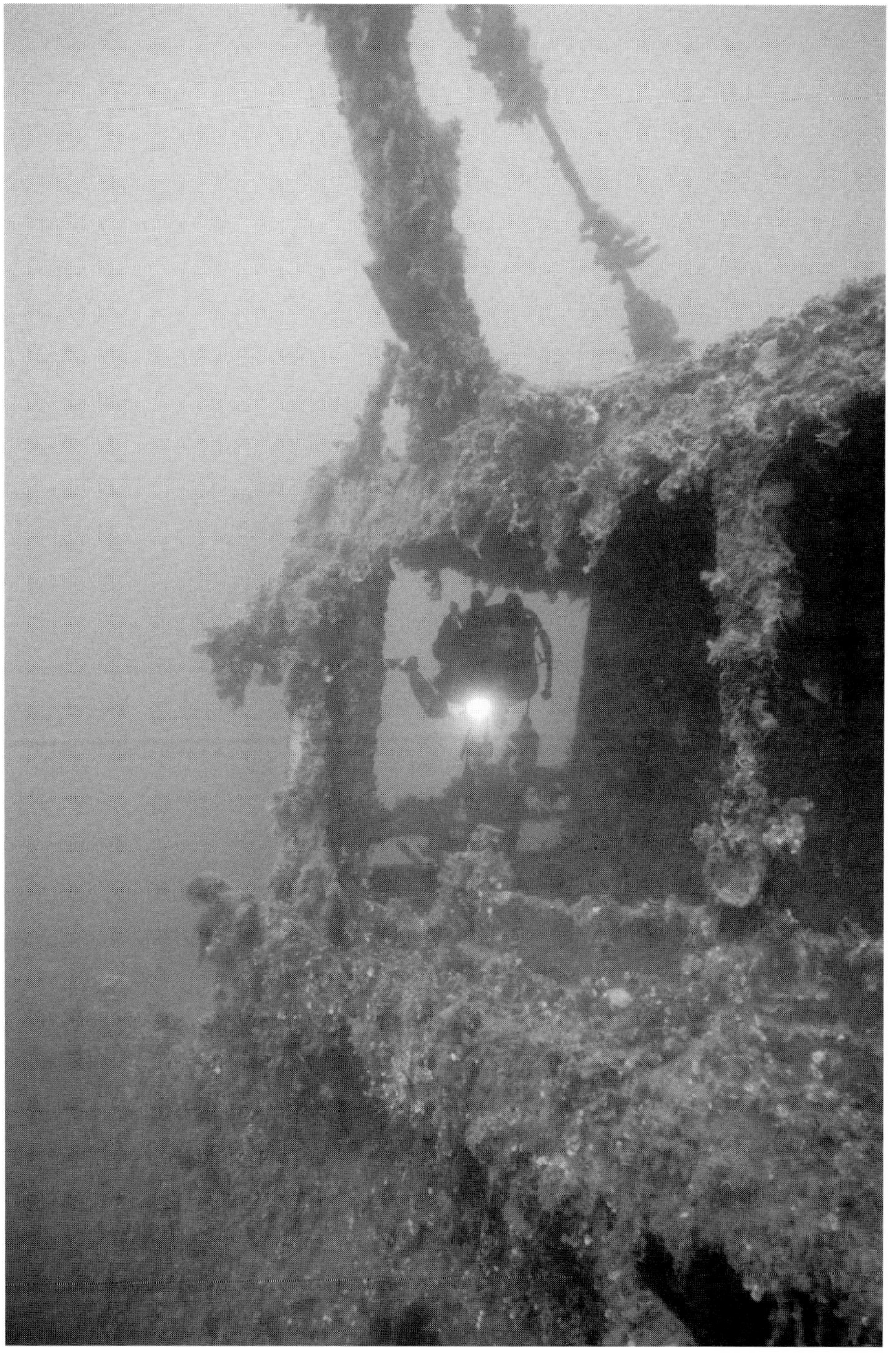

Asakazi Maru, Kwajalein Atoll,
Marshall Islands

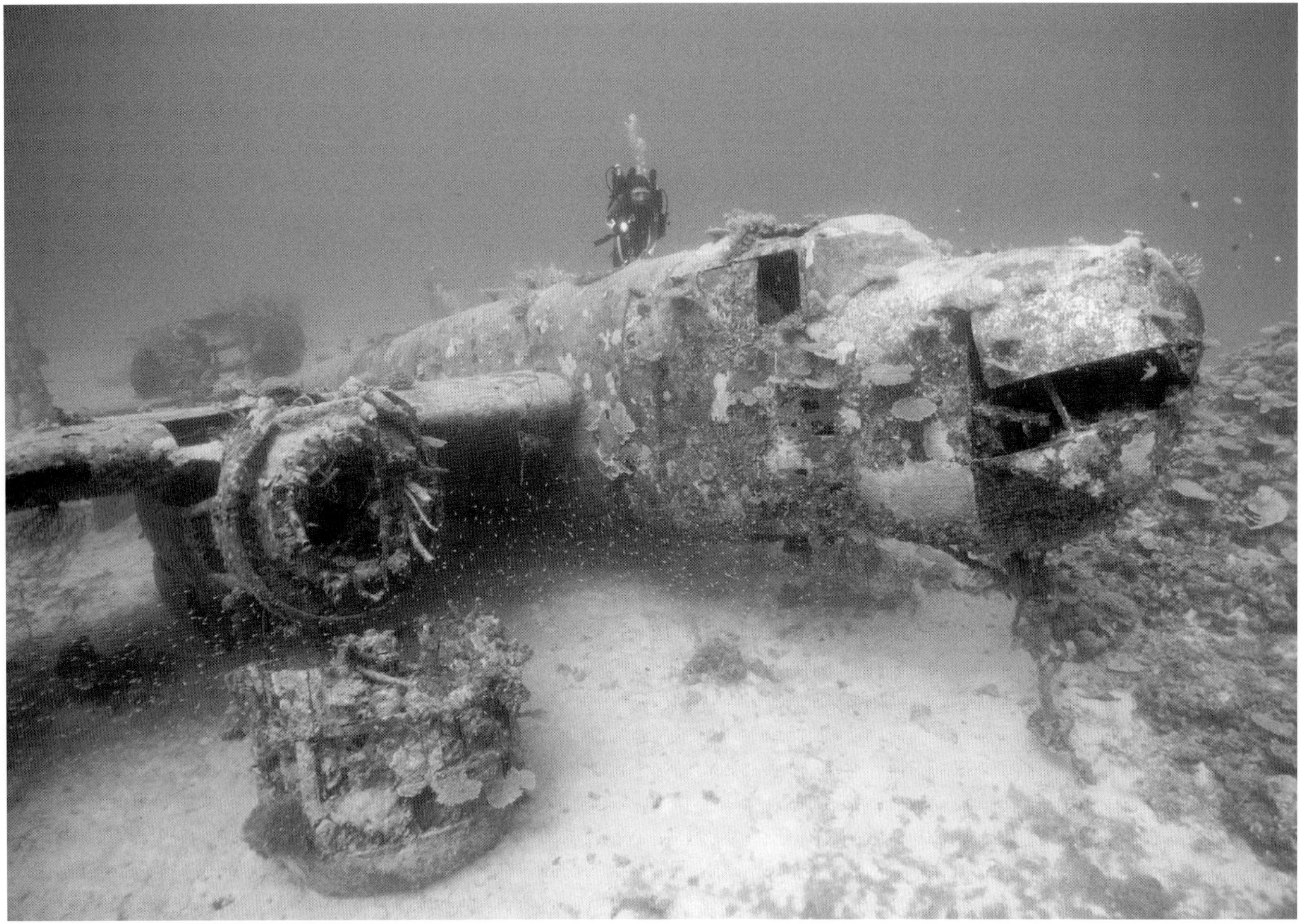

B-25 aircraft, Kwajalein Atoll, Marshall Islands

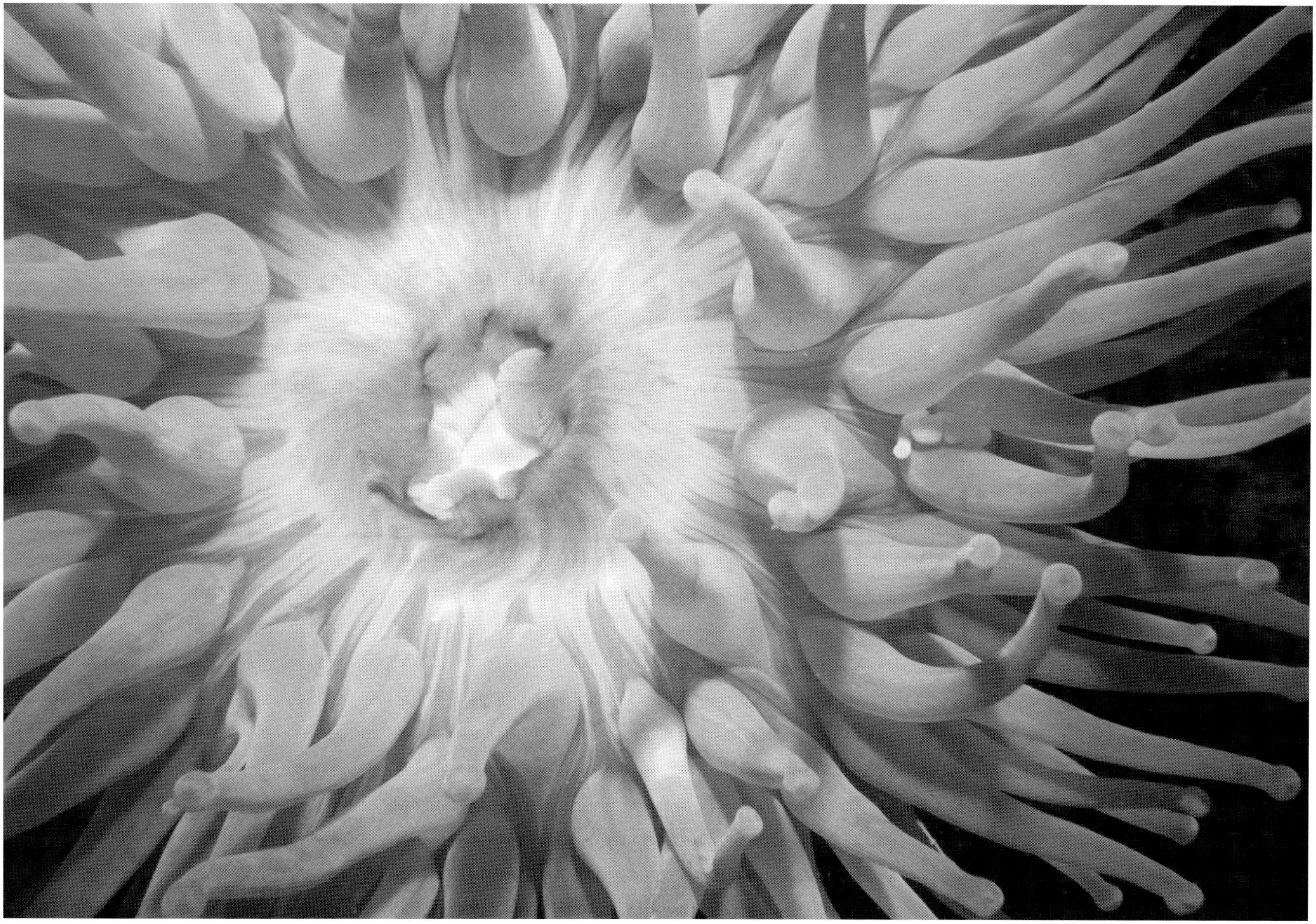

Tealia anemone, Passamaquoddy Bay, Maine

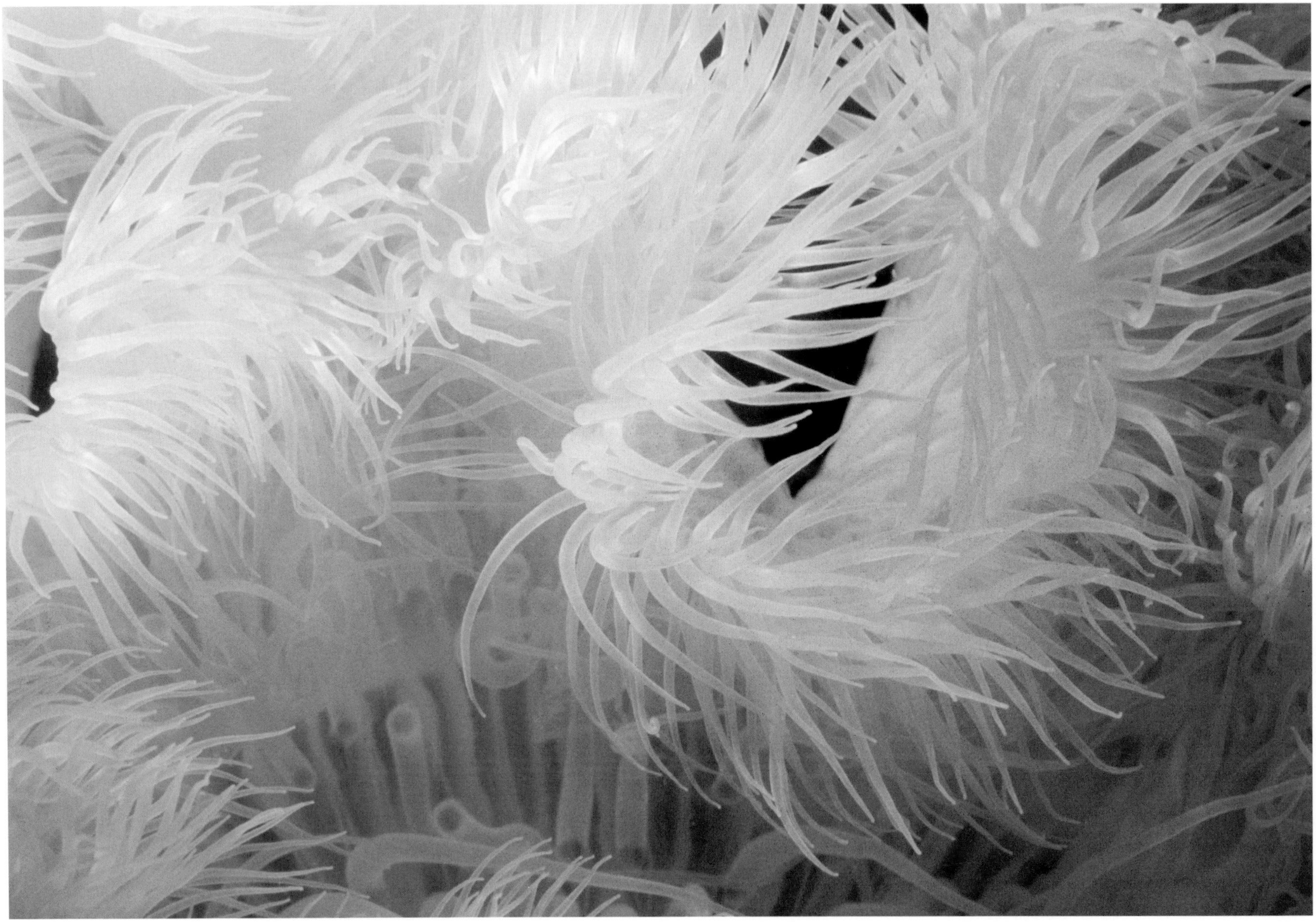

Metridium anemone, Cape Ann, Massachusetts

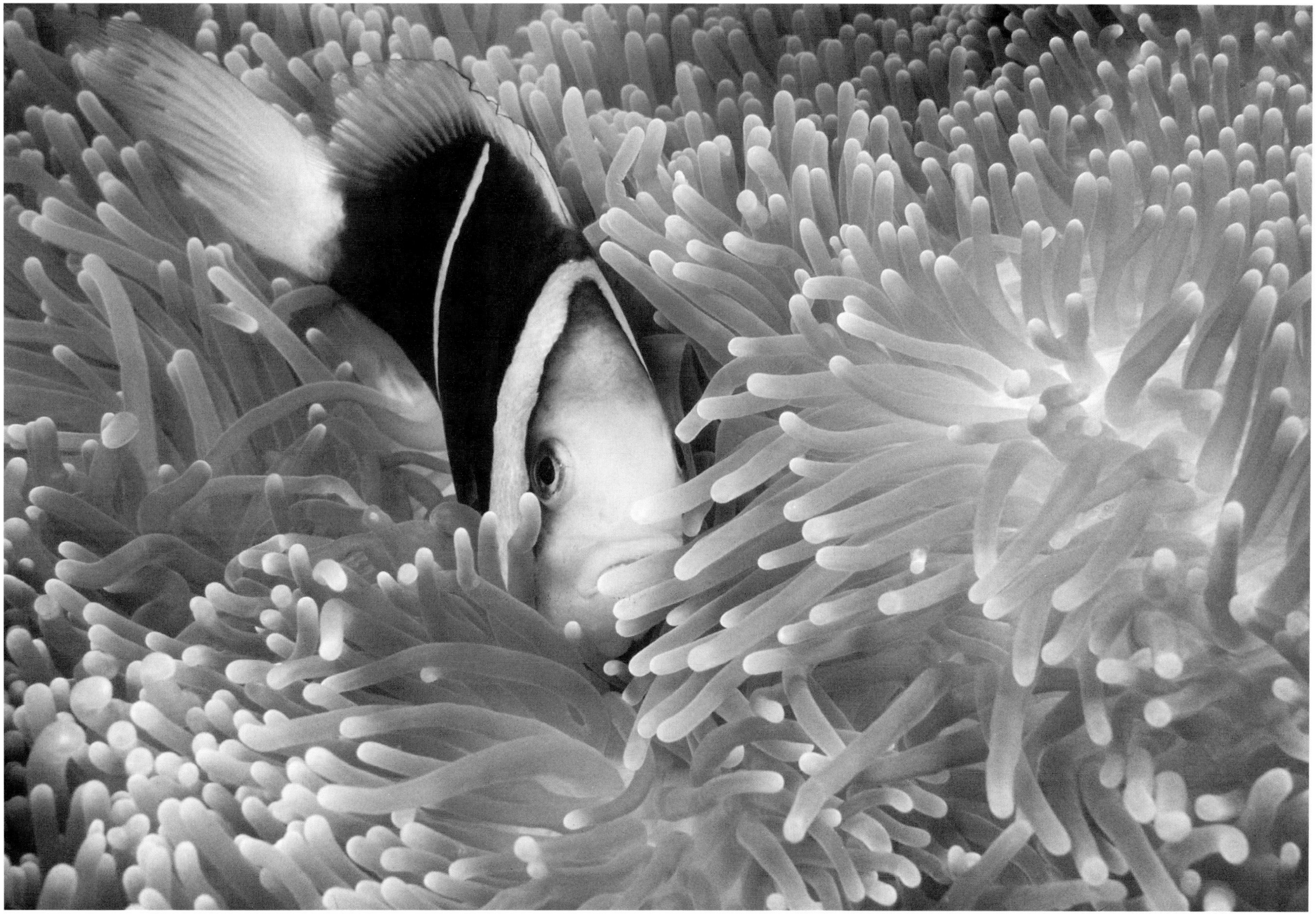

Orangefin anemonefish, Kosrae, Micronesia

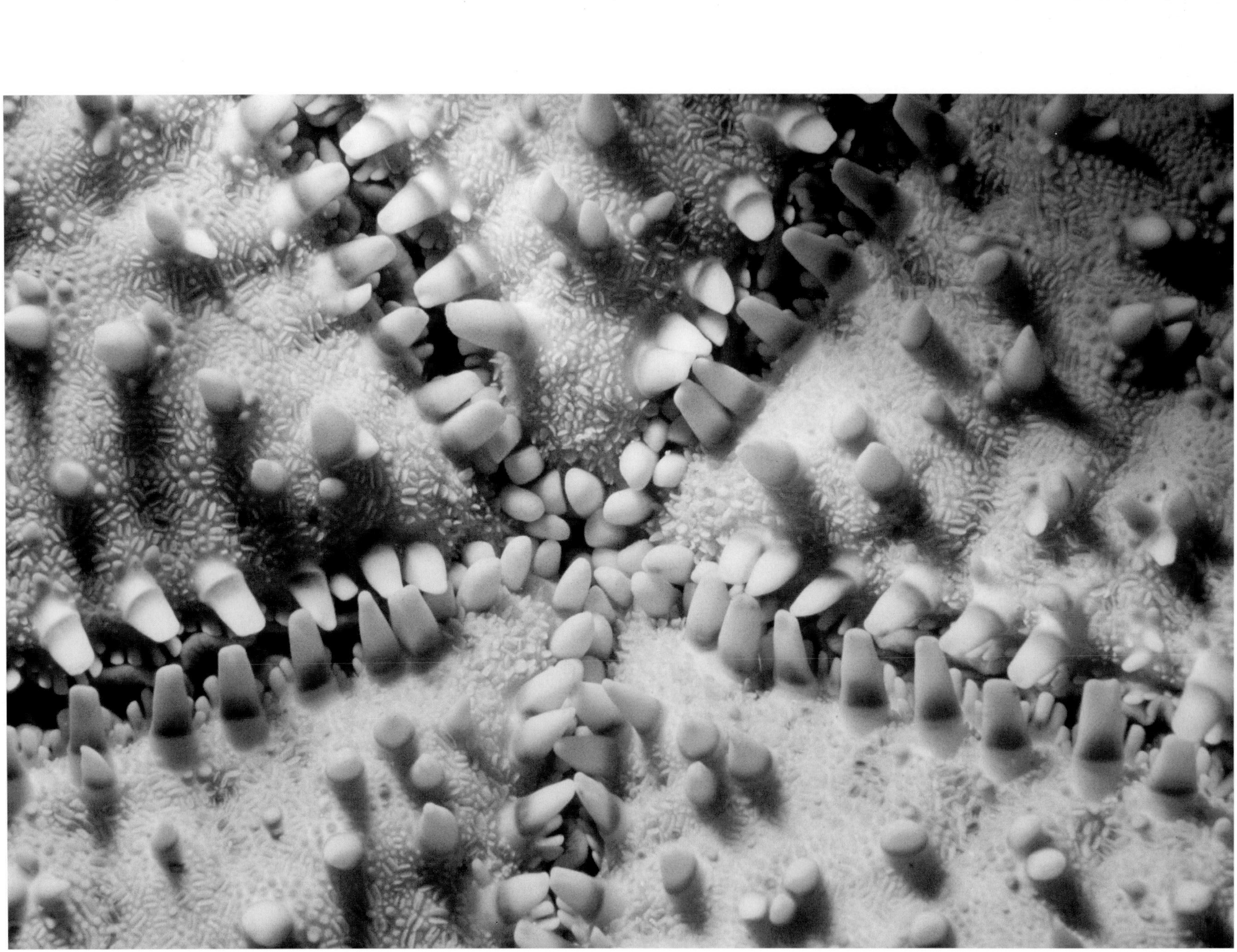

Cushion sea star, St. Croix, U.S. Virgin Islands

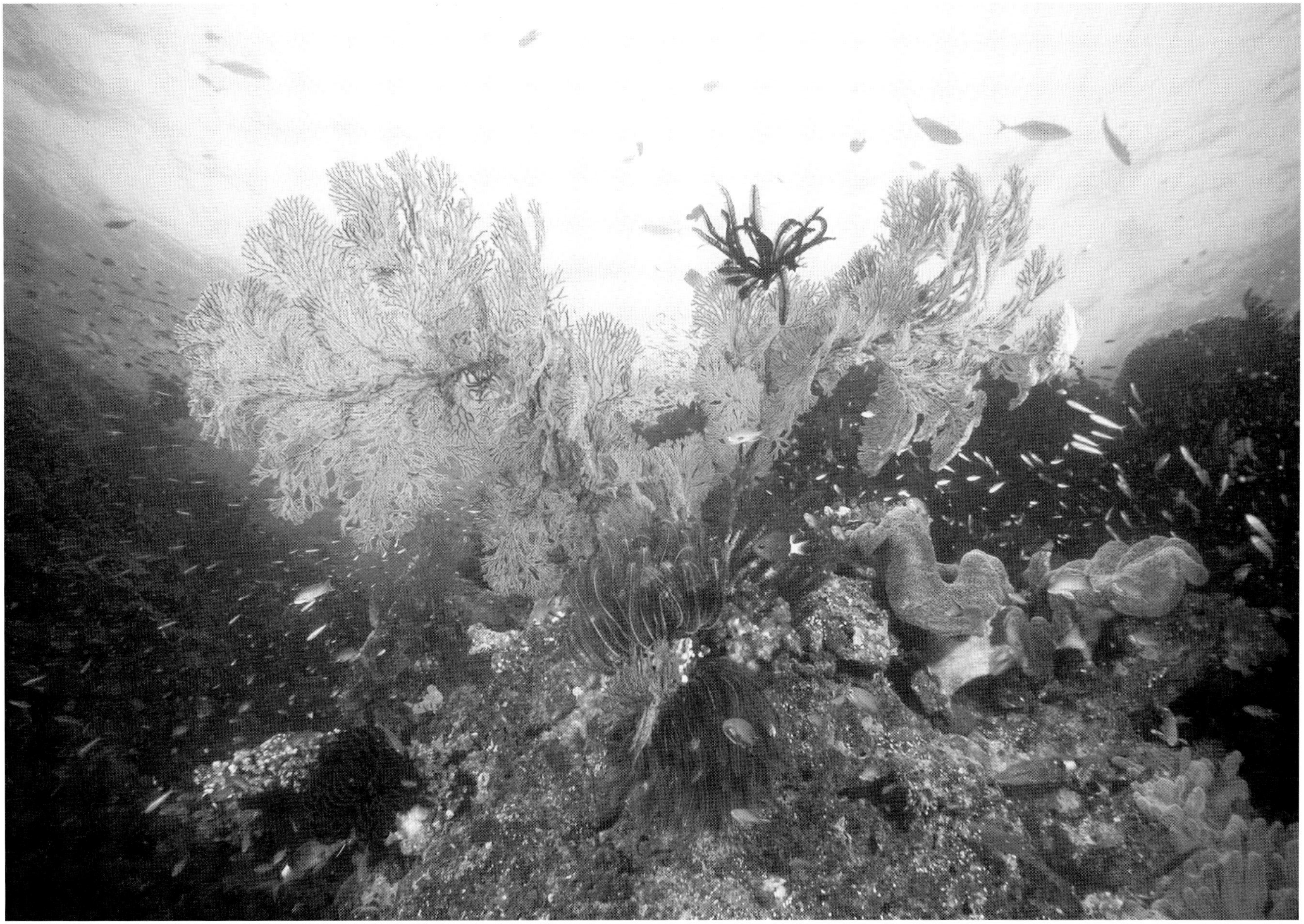

Coral reef, Fiji

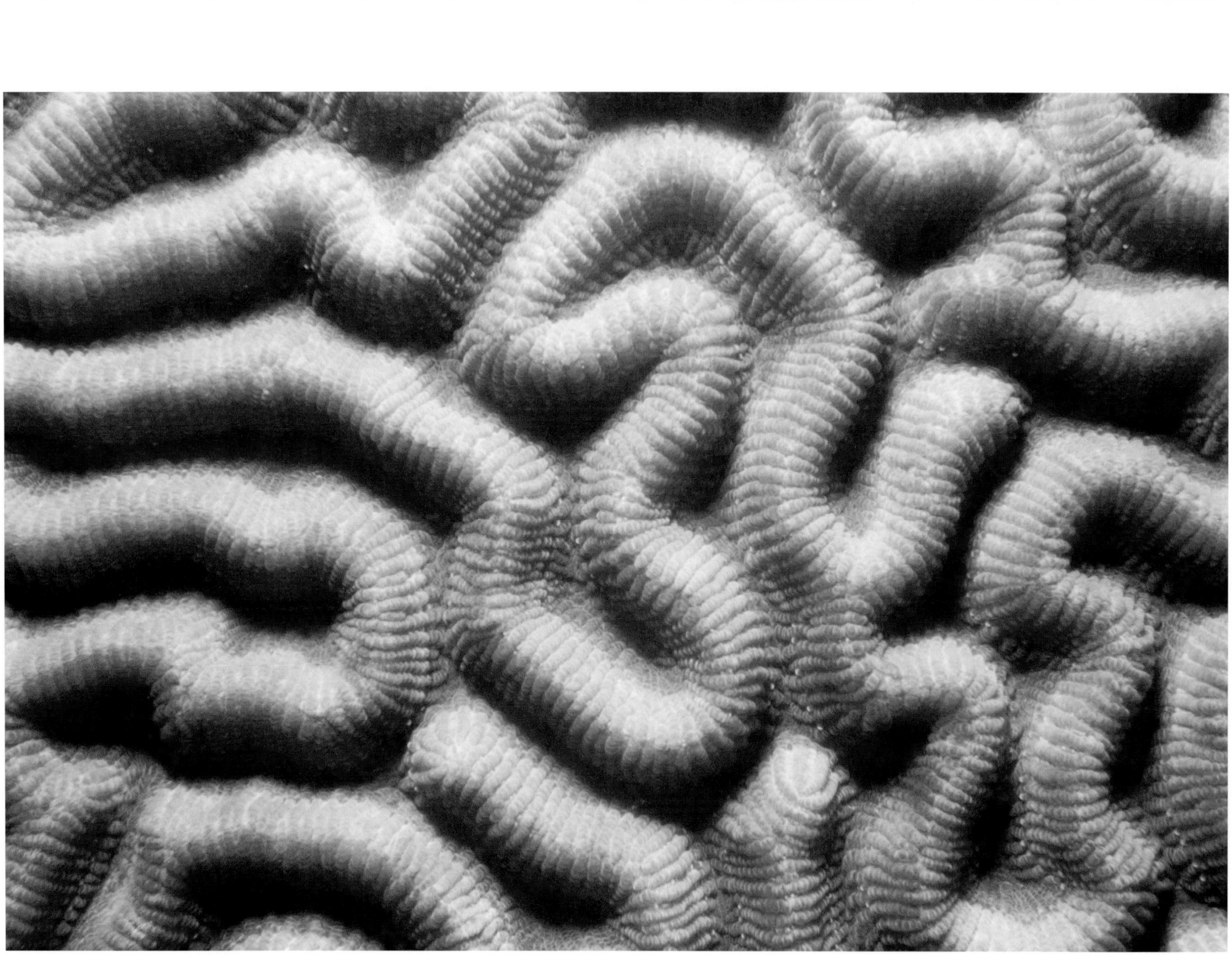

Brain coral, Cayman Islands

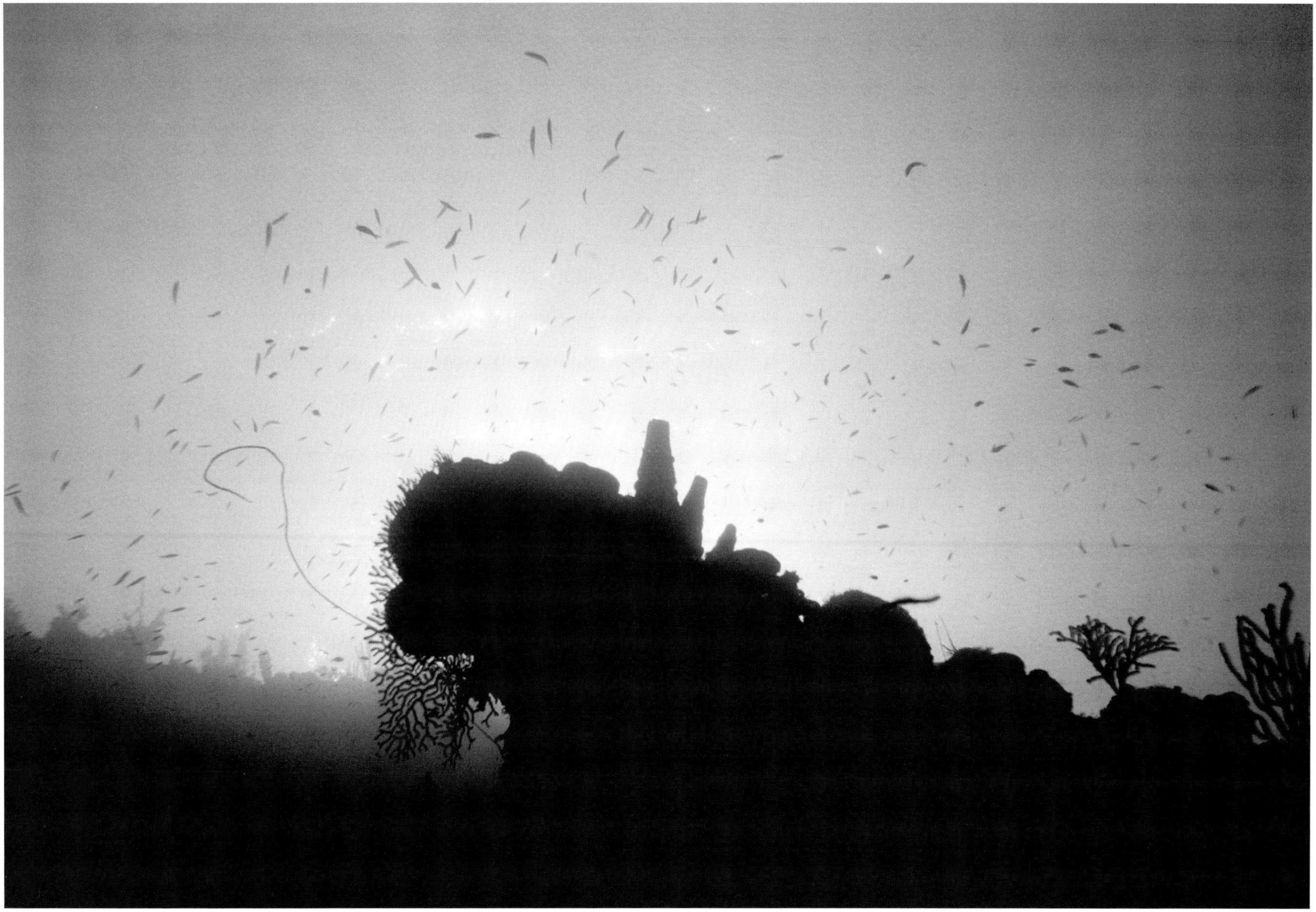

Sun and reef edge, St. Croix, U.S. Virgin Islands

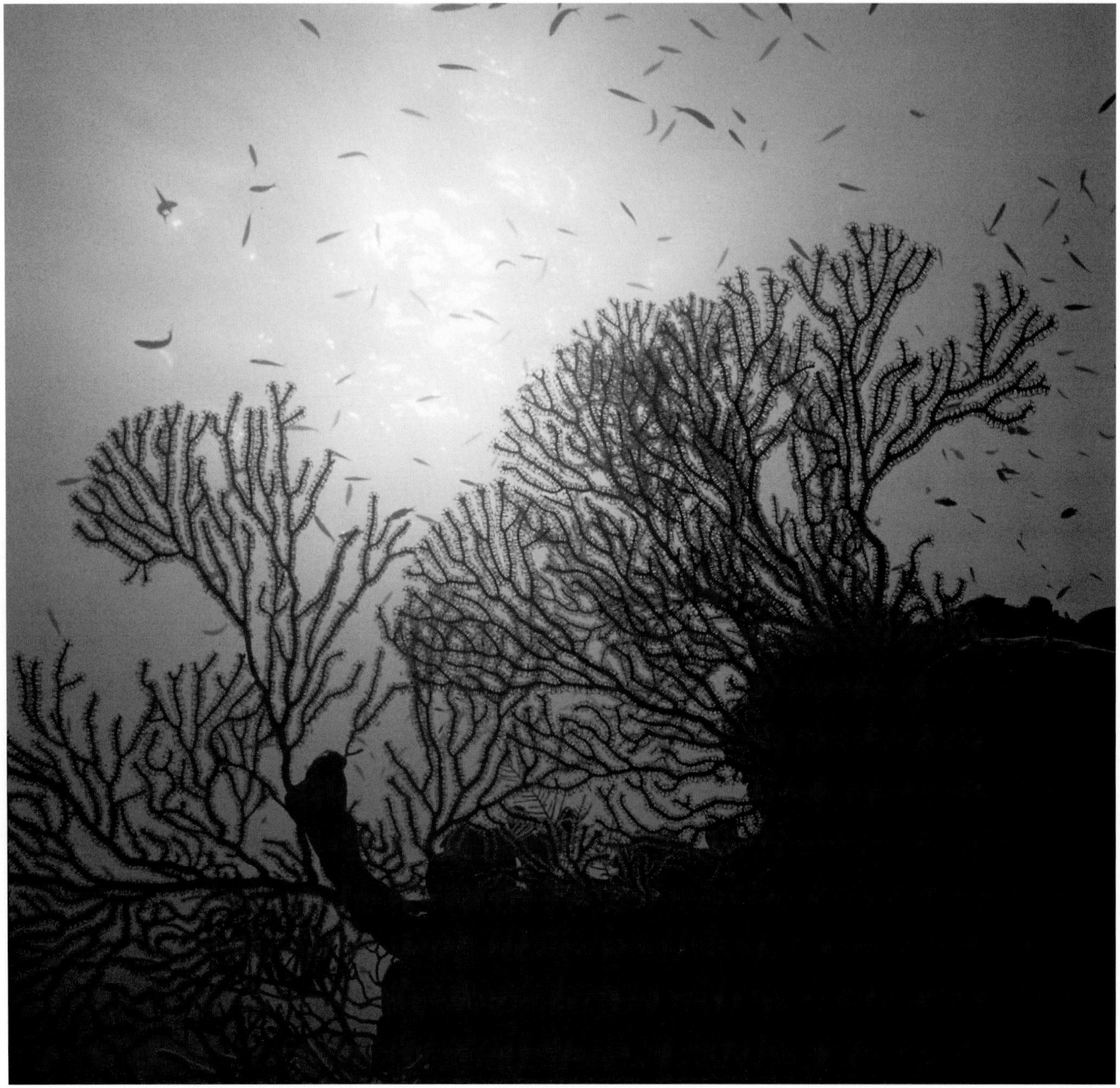

Gorgonians and sun, Turks and Caicos Islands

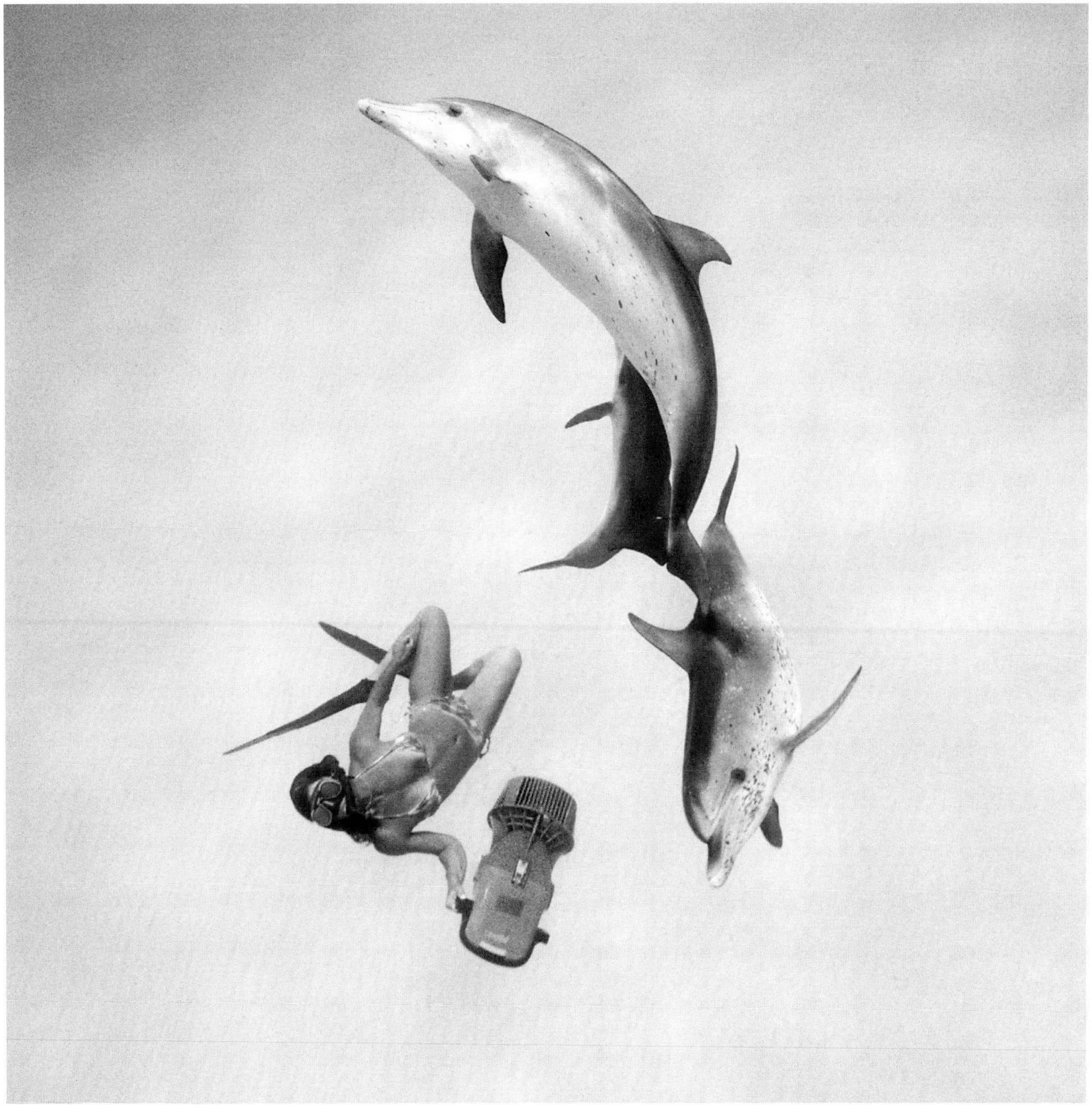

Freediver with Atlantic Spotted dolphins, Bahamas

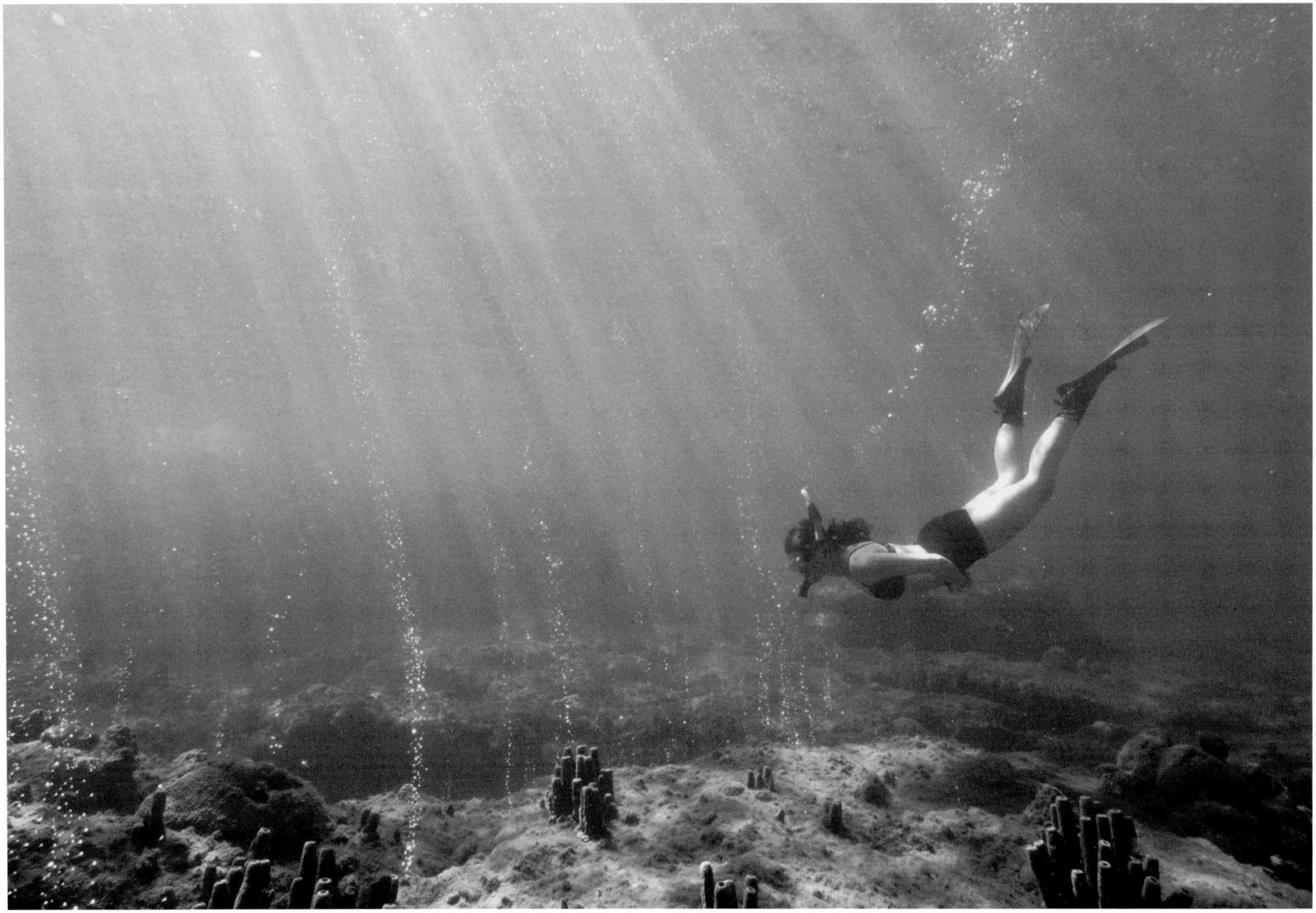

Freediver and volcanic bubbles, Dominica

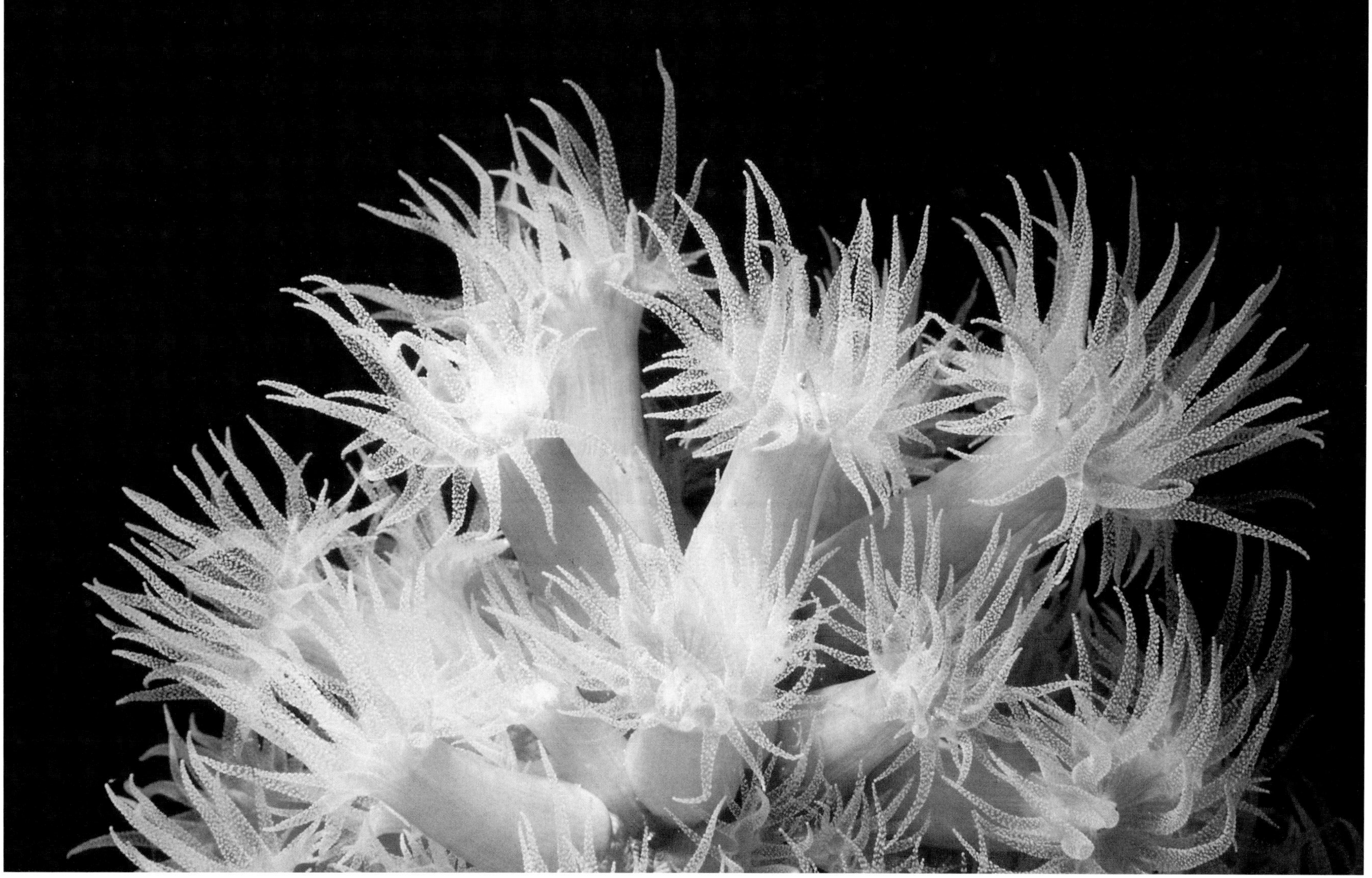

Cup coral, Bonaire

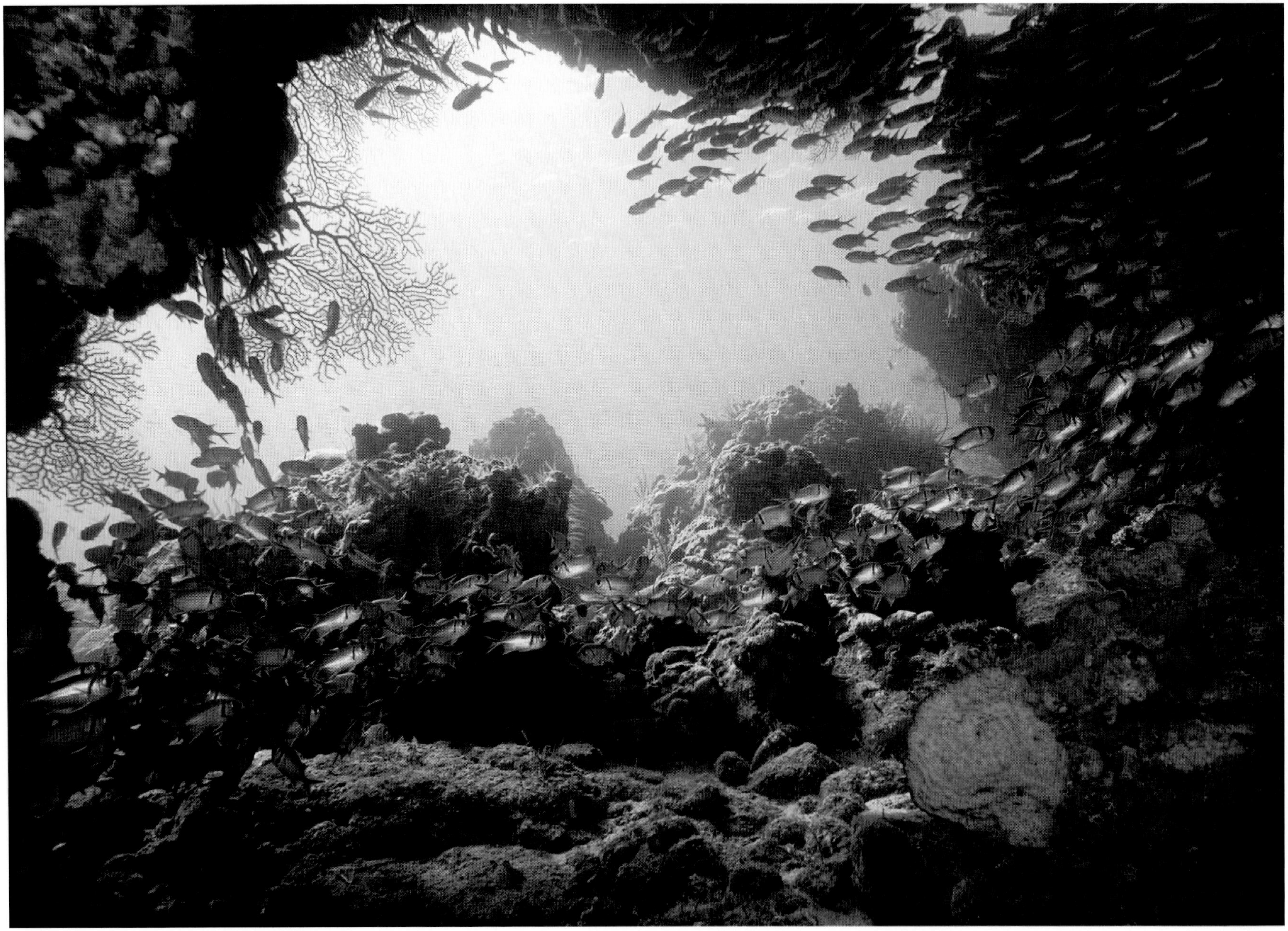

Coral cavern and Soldierfish, Dominica

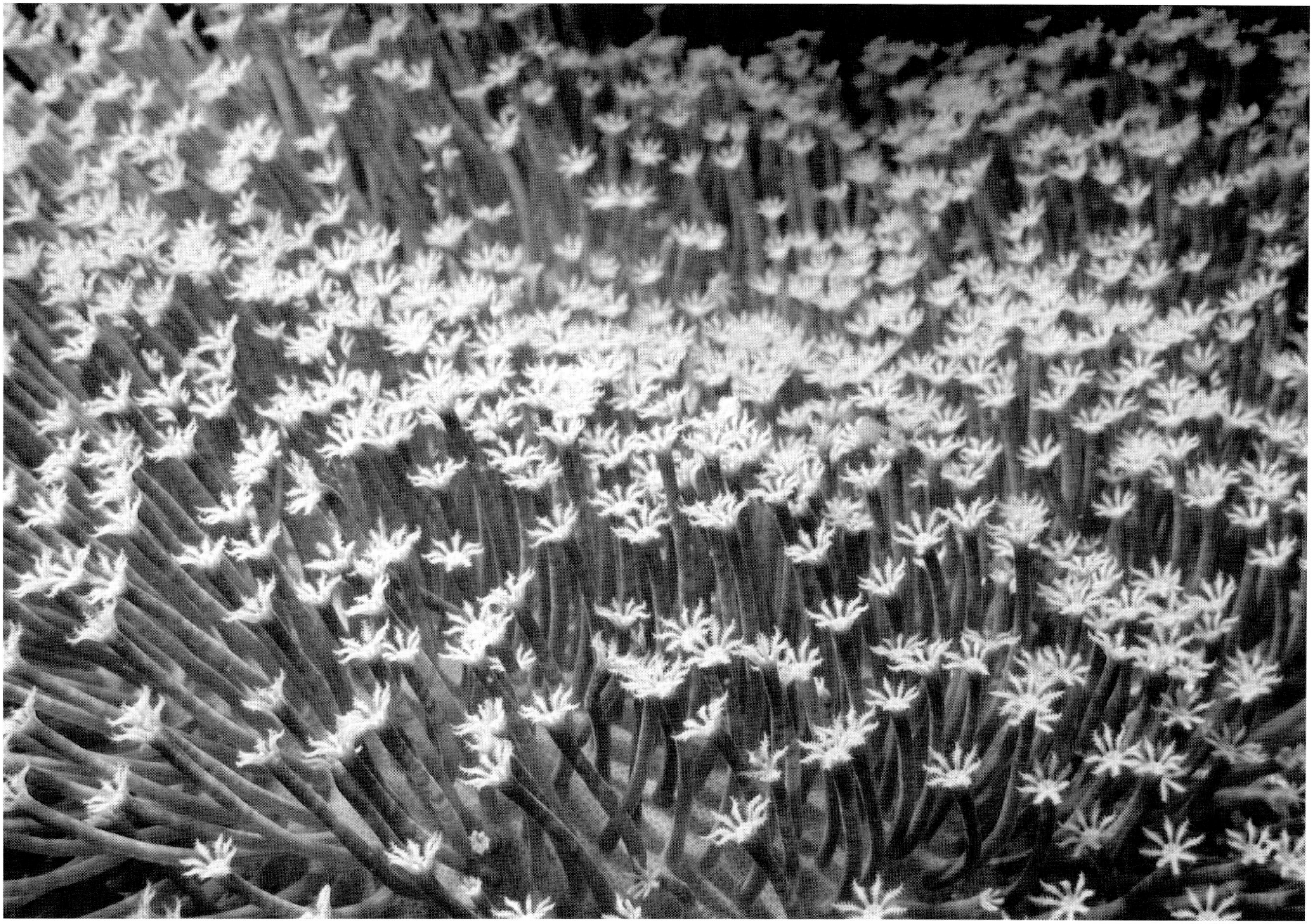

Leather coral polyps, Marshall Islands

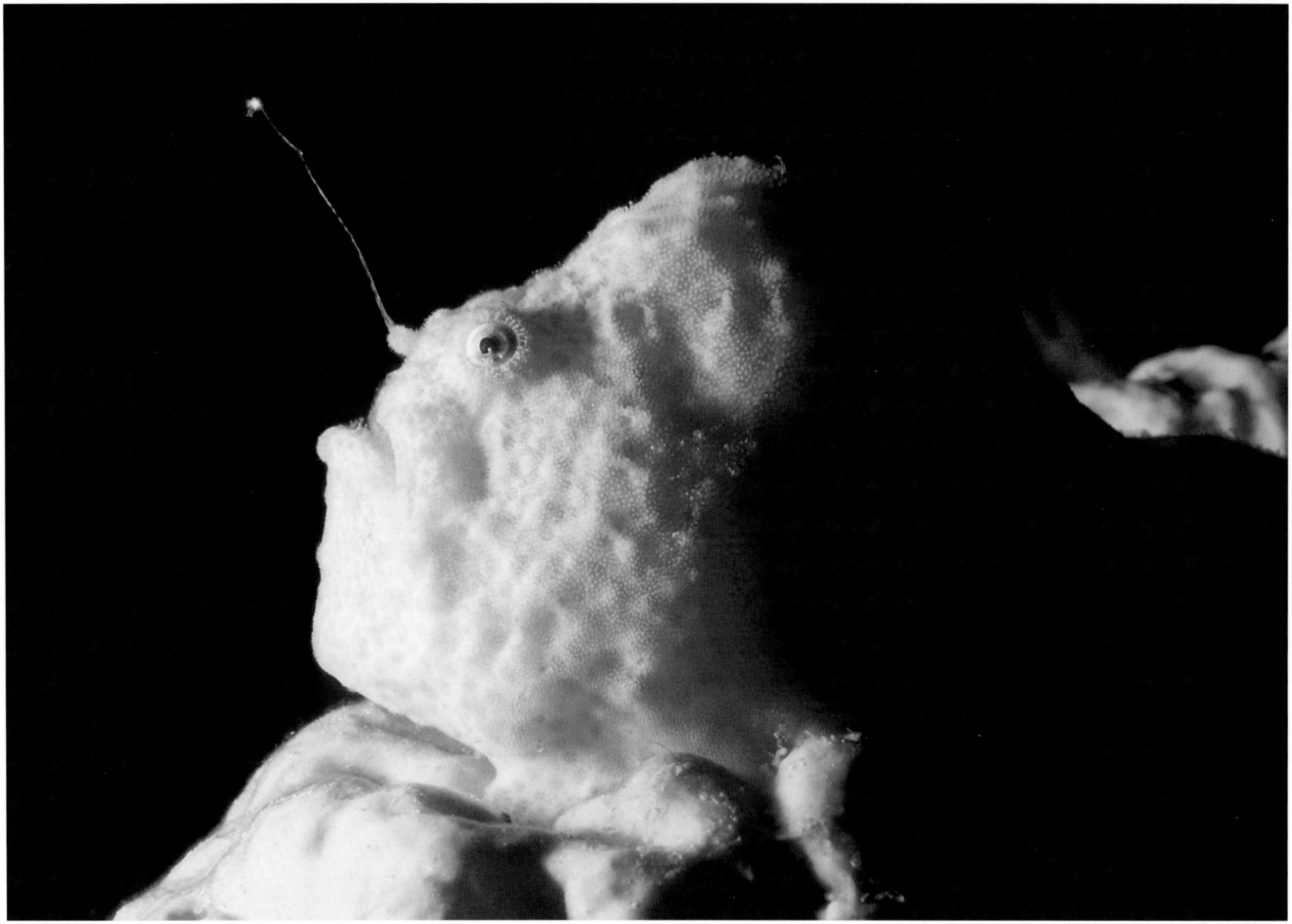

Longlure frogfish, Dominica

Notes

My interest in photography is probably genetic. My grandfather was an avid photographer, notorious with the family for his inexplicable inability to make strobe units function properly, but a splendid photographer nonetheless with a good eye for composition. As a physician, he took his hobby to work at times, producing sometimes graphic images of diseases and surgical procedures that made their way into his lectures and a few textbooks. My father and uncles got the photography bug from him. My dad brought back thousands of photographs of the conflict in Vietnam from his perspective as an Air Force pilot. In ninth grade I became interested in photography and managed to borrow my dad's old Minolta SRT-101 35 mm camera as well as my grandfather's twin lens reflex medium format camera. Immediately I had little interest in photographing people, but rather gravitated towards nature and the outdoors. My dad helped me set up a modest black and white darkroom in the bathroom and I read every book on photography and darkroom technique I could find. I discovered the works of Ansel Adams and began to truly appreciate the black and white photographic process.

In college, I worked for about a year in the black and white darkroom at a local photography studio and lab. I found it comfortable and peaceful working in the dim red glow of a safelight.

Later in college I got certified to dive and my dad gave me my first Nikonos camera as a birthday present. My first photographs underwater left a lot to be desired but I realized that the underwater world was so much more fun to photograph since it seemed like everything had already been done on land. The underwater world presented a whole new series of challenges and possibilities, but it also presented a huge array of colors. My interest in black and white photography remained on the surface as I dove to photograph the sea in color. Not for twelve years would I have much interest in the idea of underwater photography in black and white.

My eventual interest and specialization in big animal photography led me to shoot in available light quite a bit. I found these blue-hued images to resemble black and white in their monochromatic look and lack of a full color spectrum. The thought suddenly occurred to me that a lot of stuff underwater would look really great in black and white. What had I been thinking avoiding black and white for so long? Photography came full circle for me.

I am far from being alone shooting in black and white underwater. Many fine photographers have been doing it for years, yet one rarely sees much underwater black and white stuff in print. The underwater world is so filled with bizarre and abstract color, that most people are more interested in seeing the color. Nonetheless, without color you are left with only composition and lighting. Some pictures rely totally on the color—without the color, the picture becomes dull and lifeless, lacking contrast or interest. Yet many images underwater look so much more striking and surreal in black and white.

Many might find it interesting to learn that I shoot all my work on color slide film—even the black and white images in this book. Due to the limitations of underwater photography, you cannot change film or lenses underwater. When I slip over the side of the boat, I have only one lens on the camera, one roll of film and a tank of air. It never fails that when I have a macro lens, I find something too big to photograph, and when I have a wide angle lens, I find something tiny. I actually had a Humpback whale swim right by me once in the Turks and Caicos when I had a macro lens on the camera! Because the vast majority of my images get published in color, I choose to shoot on color film at all times and never chance to encounter something with incredible colors while my camera has a roll of black and white film loaded. I can always remove the color from color film by scanning it in black and white, but I can never put the color back into something shot in black and white. Some might say that this is somehow cheating, and maybe it is. It does actually *lower* my success rate at shooting good black and white images. Slide film has far less exposure latitude (tolerance for improper exposure) than black and white print film. If I shot on black and white film, I would likely have many more acceptable images than I do shooting on color reversal film, but that is the price I pay for the flexibility of being able to produce either color or black and white images from the same roll.

Part of the fun and creative process of black and white photography takes place in the darkroom. The art of dodging, burning and tweaking the image on the enlarger to produce the perfect print is often as much of a challenge as actually shooting the picture to begin with. I no longer have a traditional "wet" black and white darkroom in my home. My darkroom is now a Macintosh computer, and my digital files go to a photography lab for output to photo paper. Nothing you see in this book has been digitally manipulated beyond what one can do in a conventional darkroom (exposure adjustment, contrast, dodging and burning, cropping). I hope you enjoy the book.

Jonathan Bird

Acknowledgements

A great many people have helped me with this book along the way. I owe a great debt of thanks to: my good friends Art Cohen, Greg Brunshidle, Tim Geers, and Tom and Heather Krasuski at O.R.G.; Bob Evans and the gang at Force Fin (the best fins in the universe!); Ike Brigham, Tom Kepler, Brett Foster, Steven Koos, and Glen Goodrich, Ikelite Underwater Systems; Jules Morton and Glen Holmes; Cliff and Kathy Simoneau, C2 Expeditions; Wayne Scott Smith, Robin Sabino, Julie Pitts, Sara Dixon and Inez Smith, Dream Team; Fritz Falkner, Mike Veitch, Moses Visaka and Ropate Rakuro, Sere-ni-Wai, Fiji; Audrey Michel; My many friends on Kwajalein and Roi-Namur in the Kwajalein Scuba Club and the Roi-Namur Dolphins; Cris Merz, Galapagos Aggressor; Todd and Lynn Sisto; Charlie Donilon, Snappa Diving Charters; Al and Wendy Bozza; Jeffrey Bird, Parrelli Optical; Ty Sawyer, Pierce Hoover, Ann Louise Tuke, Kirk Brown and Gary Joyce, Sport Diver Magazine; Reneé Duncan, Alert Diver Magazine; Daryl Carson, Tiffany Carey and Ryan Allen, Skin Diver Magazine; Cathryn Castle, Dive Training Magazine; Kathy Moran, John Eliot and Chris Scaptura, National Geographic Magazine; Jay Sumner, National Geographic Kids Magazine; Susan McElhinney, Ranger Rick Magazine; Borneo Divers, Malaysia; Rick Gaffney, Destination Midway; Keoki Stender; Chris Stanton, Hidden Worlds Cenotes, Mexico; Victor Cordoba, Dressel Divers, Mexico; Dave and Sue Millhouser; Ralph and Miriam Cohn; Mary Brennan, Marcella Martinez Associates; Terry Evans and Pat Stoddard, Roatan Charters; Ken Knezick, Island Dreams Tours & Travel; Jim and Kisty Engel, Jim McClendon, Willy Waterhouse and Albert Stubbs, Utila Lodge, Honduras; Lene Petersen; Digna Dominguez and David Chinchilla, Honduras Institute of Tourism; TACA Airlines; David Gonzalez, America Central Corporation; Anthony's Key Resort, Roatan; Anse Chastanet Resort, St. Lucia; Karyn and Michael Allard, Scuba St. Lucia; Katrina Adams and Bruce Brandt, Kosrae Village Resort, Kosrae; Lance Higgs, Thorfinn, Chuuk, Micronesia; Dave Stillman and Mary Blake, Cape Ann Divers, Massachusetts; Derek and Ginette Perryman, Dave Fabian, Dive Dominica; Kurt Nose, Dominica. Finally, a big thanks to my lovely and charming wife Christine Bird for her endless enthusiasm and encouragement as well as excellent underwater modeling skills.

All photographs by Jonathan Bird.

About the Author

Jonathan Bird is a professional underwater cinematographer and photographer. He has shot and produced over 20 films for broadcast and education. His films have appeared all over the world, on networks such as PBS, ABC, USA Network, Discovery and even the SciFi Channel. He has won two Emmy Awards and two CINE Golden Eagles for his work. Jonathan is the president of Oceanic Research Group, Inc. a non-profit environmental organization, and has published articles and images in hundreds of magazines, calendars and books. He leads dive expeditions around the world and teaches underwater photography courses. More information is available at www.jonathanbird.net. Signed prints of images from this book are available.

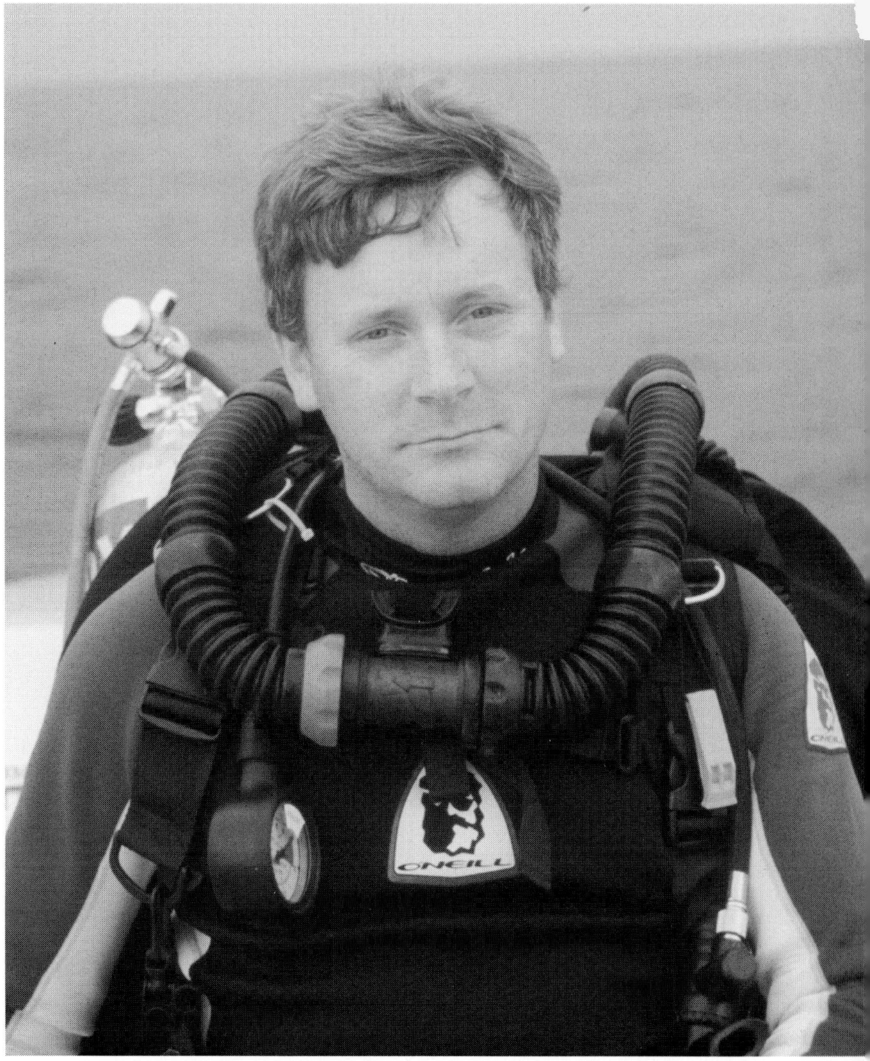